Praise for
A Beautiful Morning

"This book is for anyone who is curious about or skeptical of morning rituals. The power within all the practices and stories shared makes it real and remarkable—these rituals WORK! ... Ashley has a very light and helpful touch and approaches her topic with great joy and reverence—it feels like talking to a kind guide whose goal is simply to help your days, energy levels, health, and well-being. ... I highly recommend this, and so look forward to reading it again and again as I incorporate more ritual into my own life."

—Lauren Oujiri, life coach, poet, and author of *For Your Truth and Light: Haiku and Photography*

"The important theme that I found throughout *A Beautiful Morning* was the thread of the importance of self-care and self-compassion—giving to ourselves first, so we are at our best to give to others. This is something I believe the world strongly needs! ... I can see myself happily dipping in and out of different chapters for a refresher over time. It's a book I want to keep by my bed or desk to refer back to for inspiration in the future."

—Tracey Hewitt, artist and author of *When Your Superpower Becomes Your Kryptonite*

D1372602

a
beautiful
morning

how a morning ritual can
feed your soul and transform
your life

Ashley Ellington Brown

LEO PRESS

© 2018 by Ashley Ellington Brown. All rights reserved.

No part of this book may be used, transmitted, or reproduced in any form or by any means without written permission of the publisher or author except in the case of brief quotations embodied in critical articles and reviews.

The author and publisher assume no responsibility for any errors or omissions. No liability is assumed for damages that may result from the use of information contained within.

Published in the United States by Leo Press, Pensacola FL
Books may be purchased in quantity by visiting
www.abeautifulmorningbook.com
Library of Congress Control Number: 2017917463

Publisher's Cataloging-In-Publication Data
(Prepared by The Donohue Group, Inc.)
Names: Brown, Ashley Ellington.
Title: A beautiful morning : how a morning ritual can feed your soul and transform your life / Ashley Ellington Brown.
Description: First edition. | Pensacola FL : Leo Press, [2018]
Identifiers: ISBN 9780999510117 | ISBN 9780999510148 (ebook)
Subjects: LCSH: Women--Conduct of life. | Ritual--Psychology. | Self-actualization (Psychology) in women. | BISAC: SELF-HELP / Personal Growth / Happiness. | SELF-HELP / Self-Management / Time Management. | BODY, MIND & SPIRIT / Inspiration & Personal Growth.
Classification: LCC BF637.C5 B76 2018 (print) | LCC BF637.C5 (ebook) | DDC 158.1--dc23

Printed in the United States of America
Cover and interior design by Damonza
Editor: Jody Berman
Cover photograph © Hollytree Photo
Author photograph by Evelyn Laws Photography

For Jim and Jackson, who inspire me to be a better person and give me the courage to try.

Contents

> *"If we can sit in stillness and contemplation, it connects us to an expanded awareness and pure potentiality, and that spills over into what we do each day."*

> *"A morning ritual is important because it sets the tone and starts the day in a purposeful way. I'm centered, not rushed. ... Journaling gives me time to think about what's going on and listen to God."*

> *"Meditation helps me to be aware of my thoughts and handle them before I react. [It] has a very positive effect, but it can be subtle. At first, the benefits aren't obvious; then you realize, 'Oh, I'm calmer and less short-tempered when I do it regularly!'"*

> *"Overall, I think the most vital thing is taking quiet time for yourself. That's when you hear your own voice and find your own truth."*

> *"Doing a sixty-second ritual every day will give you a lot more bang for your buck than doing a three-hour ritual once or twice."*

> *"I used to wake up and think about work right away, which was stressful. Now I've created this habit of being thankful first thing instead, and it's a much better way to start my day."*

> *"Self-care helps me access my intuition and gives me clarity."*

Prologue

LIVING MINDFULLY IS a way to honor and care for ourselves. We are not workhorses to be whipped into productivity each day. We are luminous souls who deserve to enjoy the gorgeous experience of being human.

We spend much of our lives on autopilot and can end up in a life we didn't consciously create. Taking a moment through a morning ritual to pay attention can produce incredible results. Self-awareness helps us see what's working in our lives and what's not—what nourishes us and what drains us.

Being still opens the lines of communication to our inner selves and clears the way for what have been called "divine downloads." It could be a thunderbolt ("I want to change careers") or a tiny realization ("I've actually never liked coffee—I prefer tea"). Large or small, momentous or infinitesimal, these insights nevertheless guide us toward our true selves and what will fulfill us. They show us what course corrections are necessary to reach our ultimate goals. They show us what our ultimate goals truly are!

This book is here in your hands because of just such an insight.

I was sitting in my backyard one beautiful spring morning, basking in sunshine and birdsong and appreciating how much my new morning ritual was enhancing my life. Instead of rushing around frantically, I was consciously taking time for myself. As a result, I felt calmer, happier, and more energized.

I had just started a telecourse led by Martha Beck called Write into Light. I began wondering how she started her day—surely she had some lovely, powerful rituals! Then I started thinking of other inspiring women and wondered about their morning rituals. And then I thought, "Hmmm, that would be a fascinating book."

I decided to interview women I admire—who are following their dreams and creating lives that fulfill them—about their morning rituals so I could share this life-changing magic with others. Many months later, here is my divine download in physical form, and I am immensely grateful. Enjoy!

Introduction

IMAGINE YOU ARE the world's greatest surfer. You float peacefully on your board as the rising sun sparkles across the water. A wave comes toward you; you're calmly confident and ready to ride it. In one graceful motion you're up and perfectly balanced. You skim over the water to the gleaming sand, leap off, and rest a moment in the gentle surf. Then you paddle back out with vigor to ride the next wave.

When your life is going smoothly, it feels like you're surfing—gliding gloriously along, powerful and in control. Starting each day with purpose through a personally meaningful morning ritual can give you that effortless sensation. Cultivating an inner core of strength and serenity helps you surf through life's ups and downs with confidence and ease.

Enhance your ability to *be*

Most books and articles about morning rituals focus on enhancing your productivity—your ability to *do*. This book is about enhancing your ability to *be*. Productivity is marvelous, but to be calm and centered *while* you're productive—that is the essence of a happy life.

We want what we're doing to reflect who we truly are. We are not our roles—daughter, wife, mother, friend, boss, employee, volunteer, grandmother—we are our *selves*. If we don't take the time to listen to ourselves and learn what we truly want, all that doing will drain us dry. It will put us squarely in the middle of a life that doesn't nourish us.

Focus on what works for *you*

This book is about giving yourself space to discover what makes you happiest. Just you—not your parents or your spouse or anyone else who has opinions about what you "should" do with your life. It does not provide a strict regimen that you must follow or you'll fail. There is no "doing it right." Even if all you ever manage is to sit for a minute and gaze out the window while you drink your coffee—or breathe deeply a few times while you're taking your shower—you will have "succeeded." None of us needs anything more to stress about!

As you'll see in the following pages, you do not have to get up at 4:00 a.m. to get the life you want. If you like to get up early, wonderful. If not, you can still create a ritual that will have a positive impact on your life.

Do what feeds your soul

Use the information and ideas offered here as guidance to create a morning ritual that is unique to you. One size does not fit all, as the women interviewed in this book clearly demonstrate. Some exercise first thing in the morning; others like to meditate. Some snuggle up with tea and a journal; others go for a walk or do yoga. Some rituals take five minutes; others might take an hour or more.

The women you will meet range in age (from twenties to seventies), occupation, and life circumstance; each one has carefully crafted her ritual to meet her needs. Let them inspire you to do the same. Read through their stories. See what resonates with you, and what new ideas are sparked. I was fascinated with the variations from person to person, and I think you will be too.

Why in the morning?

Every morning presents an opportunity for a fresh start. When we wake up, we can choose our mindset. If the previous day didn't please us, we can try something new today. It's like pressing the reset button—and we get that chance every twenty-four hours. We can make new choices every day.

The morning sets the tone for the rest of the day. If we create an oasis of calm through a morning ritual, we can carry that feeling within us, greatly increasing the chances that we will have a peaceful and positive day. This is especially important for women. We tend to get up and immediately start handling outside obligations, whether it's for family or work. If we take a moment to care for ourselves first, we fill our own well and have more to give.

A morning ritual is one of the highest forms of self-care. We're literally putting ourselves first. When we do this each morning, it helps train us to put ourselves first throughout our life. This is not selfish, it's necessary. If we keep putting others' needs ahead of our own, never taking the time to replenish our reserves, we will eventually run out. A morning ritual refuels us every day, keeping our life running smoothly.

Realizing this, and incorporating a morning ritual, has changed my life. Until recently, I would sleep as late as possible and race to get ready. Not surprisingly, my days felt hectic. I was always running to catch up. This made me impatient and irritable. I felt like I never had time to do what *I* wanted, which led to feeling resentful. And I was tired. No matter how much I slept, I was always tired.

Finally, I realized I was wasting my very short precious life and decided to change. I began investigating how to live more peacefully and joyfully. I read dozens of books, took quite a few courses, and worked with several amazing coaches.

Along the way, I picked up tips about starting the day mindfully and how it could impact my life positively. Intrigued, I began with the tiniest of steps: stretching while still in bed, taking some deep belly breaths, and mentally repeating "peace" a few times. I was astonished at how much of a difference that teensy change made.

I decided to try waking up a little earlier—just thirty minutes—so I could fit in a few more things. It has truly been amazing. I am more engaged and enthusiastic, more calm and centered, and more clear and focused. When there are difficult days, I seem to be able to handle them better.

Why "ritual"?

I chose the word "ritual" thoughtfully. "Practice" implies trying, or work. The last thing we need is more work in our lives! Many of us are tired of trying so hard all the time, striving for success on every level. No striving here.

"Ritual" is special. A ritual is sacred. It elevates the ordinary and the simple—just consider the Japanese tea ceremony. A ritual is performed slowly, with attention and gratitude. It calms.

I invite you to treat yourself while you read this book. Play with creating a ritual around it. Snuggle up somewhere cozy. Make a cup of tea or pour a glass of wine. Light a candle or put on some good music. Browse through the book with a peaceful mind and open heart. Relax into a sense of possibility and ease open a window onto a new view of your life.

Taking time for yourself benefits others

If you think it sounds selfish to take time for yourself when you have responsibilities to others, consider how it can actually help them. When your energy is calm, you emanate peace, and that influences those around you. As you go about your day, you can leave serenity in your wake, uplifting your loved ones, friends, coworkers—even strangers.

If you doubt this, consider the opposite. Have you ever been near someone who was furious or overcome with grief? Could you feel their emotions? Our moods are contagious, and the world could really use more positive energy these days. You're performing a service by spreading good vibes!

To consciously cultivate peace in yourself in order to share it with others is a noble pursuit indeed.

What benefits can a morning ritual give you?

A path to happiness

We all want to feel good. That desire is at the root of everything humans do. But if we aren't clear about what truly makes us feel good—if we don't listen to our inner voice but get distracted by fears and others' opinions—we can get pulled along by external forces, guided onto a path we didn't completely choose. We react to situations rather than being proactive. We race from obligation to obligation, putting out fires we didn't start, getting more and more overwhelmed.

Creating a morning ritual is about taking charge of our day from the very beginning, gently, with purpose. When we start the day on our own terms, we are better prepared to live our lives that way. We are mindful and calm. We can see more clearly the path that we genuinely desire to take—the path that leads to our happiest, most fulfilled life.

Better focus and more serenity

You would think we would feel calm first thing in the morning. But for many of us, our mind starts racing the minute we open our eyes. Planning the day, worrying about problems, fearing events that may never happen … it's nonstop.

When was the last time you actually felt the warm water in your shower or were really aware that you were brushing your teeth? Our bodies automatically get us ready while our minds run us ragged. Before we get to work or start our chores at home—often before we've even had our coffee—we are worn out. Scattered thoughts scatter our energy.

When I start my day with a morning ritual, I'm better able to focus my attention on one thing at a time. I am more present, which makes me more productive. I handle what's in front of me instead of worrying about the future or agonizing about the past. After all, the present moment is all we actually have. Neither the past nor the future is under our control. All we can affect is our current reality.

By putting our mind and body in a state of serenity first thing in the morning, we make it easier to stay there throughout the day. If something happens to throw us off course, it's easier to get back. Life's turbulence can wash over us but not take us under. We respond and adjust as needed, but we're not overwhelmed. It's like cocooning ourselves in a cashmere blanket; it softens the impact of any adversity. We're able to live by the slogan I have on my fridge: "When things go wrong, don't go with them."

Improved relationships

If we're in good spirits when we first greet our family members and coworkers, as opposed to being preoccupied or aggravated, it can do wonders for our relationships. Also, being more present is hugely beneficial. When we pay attention to the person we're with, listening to what they say rather than thinking about our to-do list, they can tell. We have deeper, more genuine connections, and those lead to a richer, fuller life.

When we commit to a morning ritual, we're honoring ourselves. By taking the time to listen to our inner voice, we're showing ourselves that we matter. We're acknowledging that we have needs. We're offering love and attention to ourselves so that we can then provide love and attention to others. When we are kind to ourselves, we act more kindly toward others, and they in turn will act more kindly toward us. Kindness begets kindness.

When we show ourselves love, that love is magnified and attracts more. We become like a little sun, glowing from our own source and shining that energy on others. We are more accepting, more generous, more enthusiastic, and more playful, and we bring out those qualities in others.

A morning ritual can help us realize we are connected with everyone and that separation is just an illusion. This fosters a sense of empathy and compassion. When we approach others with compassion, it creates interactions that are more open, more sincere, and more worthwhile for both parties.

More joy

The world is full of joy and our lives can be too, if we hold space open for it. Sitting quietly, walking in nature, writing—these rituals hold that space open. They give our soul a chance to breathe, a respite from the incessant chatter of the mind. We can relax into the present moment like sinking into a warm bubble bath, and we can take delight in what we find there.

We approach the day with openness, which helps us grow and reveals the choices we want to make—how to achieve what our heart desires. We act from a place of authenticity, rather than fear or unconscious reaction, and this will lead us on the path to the life that is right for us. When we are living aligned with what we truly want, we are joyful, and the joy we feel flows out to others.

Clarity and inspiration

Women often have difficulty achieving the lives of our dreams. In fact, we often have difficulty even knowing what our dreams are. Centering ourselves with a morning ritual helps us access that inner knowing. By connecting to our core self, the one who is often drowned out by the world, we are able to know ourselves better and see clearly what it is that we want. Then we can map out how to achieve it.

Insight bubbles up when the mind is still. Clarity can come in through the window that quiet opens. When we stop bombarding ourselves with opinions, projections, and fears, we can access our intuition. When we give ourselves time without distraction, with the world shut out and our mundane thoughts muted, we can hear what the quiet voice of our soul whispers.

A morning ritual creates the space for inspiration to come to us. We can realize solutions to problems and receive insights about ourselves and others that will make our life easier.

How to use this book

Feel free to read this book from beginning to end or flip through and pick out the chapters that look most interesting to you. As you learn about what others do, aspects of their rituals may call to you. You may want to make notes in a journal as you read; you can also use sticky notes to mark meaningful sections. This will help you later as you create your own ritual.

I've placed a section at the end of each chapter called "Take a Moment." This space will serve as a gentle reminder to pause, take a breath, and remember that each woman has built her ritual over time, through trial and error. It's also a chance to pay attention to your reactions and take some notes, which will guide you as you begin to think about your own ritual and what it might look like. What attracted you? What seemed like fun? What seemed like too much effort? It's helpful to write down what you liked—*and* what you didn't. Knowing what you *don't* want can often help you figure out what you *do* want.

Many of the women mention tools they use. In the Resources section, I've included a list of these with links for more information.

Use this book to help you craft a ritual that will feed *your* soul, fit into the life *you* have, and help you create the life of *your* dreams. In chapter 22 (Creating Your Own Beautiful Morning), the appendixes, and the Resources section, you will find additional guidance and ideas to assist you.

I had such fun talking to all the fascinating women in this book. They speak so eloquently about their rituals. I've kept the stories in their own voices so it's like they're talking to you, too. If you would like to learn more about them, you'll find their website addresses in the Resources section. You will also find live links and some wonderful pictures of them and their rituals at www.abeautifulmorningbook.com.

I hope you enjoy reading about the incredible variety of morning rituals as much as I enjoyed writing about them, and that you come away with at least one spark that inspires your mornings to be beautiful and your life to be exactly as you want it!

Note to the Reader

If you're looking for specific ideas to suit your interests, here's a quick guide that may help you.

If you're not a morning person:
Chapters 5, 10, 18, 20, 21

If you like to exercise:
Chapters 4, 8, 9, 11, 13, 15, 17, 19, 21

If you like to write:
Chapters 1, 2, 3, 5, 10, 12, 17, 20, 21

If you enjoy nature:
Chapters 1, 8, 10, 14, 15, 20

If you're interested in meditation:
Chapters 1, 3, 6, 8, 9, 10, 11, 12, 14, 15, 16, 17, 18, 19, 20, 21

If you're interested in spirituality:
Chapters 2, 6, 8, 10, 12, 17, 18, 19, 21

If you enjoy creativity/art/music:
Chapters 2, 3, 6, 7, 15, 17, 18, 21

If you have children at home:
Chapters 2, 5, 11, 16, 20, 21

1

Carla Robertson

CARLA IS A Martha Beck Certified Master Life Coach who
specializes in nature-based coaching, including wilderness
retreats, through her company Living Wild and Precious. She
lives in New Orleans, Louisiana, with her husband and cats.

*"When I take time to meditate or sit outside,
starting my morning slowly and with intention, it
makes a real difference. It helps me connect with
my essential self and sets the tone for the day. I
have more compassion … For example, when I'm
crossing the street, rather than seeing the traffic, I'll
look at each person driving and think, 'Oh, I hope
you have a nice morning.'"*

I don't follow the same ritual every day; for me it's like choosing from a menu. What I do depends on the weather, the day's agenda, what I did the night before, and what I'm feeling emotionally. I love getting up early enough to have time to pad around the house and do what I want before I have any obligations. It makes me feel free.

Sometimes I wake up despondent and feel like everything's too hard, so I'll take it easy on myself and go slow. Other days I might wake up very early—like 4:30 a.m.—and not be able to go back to sleep. Instead of being aggravated, I'll go ahead and get up. It can be helpful just to start working, especially if it's dark. Usually I'll write. Then I'll feel like, "Okay, now I'm ahead of the day and can settle in once the sun comes up."

If everything is going beautifully, I often begin with meditation. I'll sit outside or with the doors open if the weather is nice. When it's cold, I might sit in bed. I like being flexible and choosing what feels right in that moment.

Connecting with nature is my favorite thing to do. I like to go out to my yard, sit on the ground, and just be. How long I sit varies. When I do this, I'm not meditating per se—I'm observing nature and sitting in wonder. If I'm feeling out of sorts or overwhelmed, I tend to withhold nature time from myself. I have to remember to be kind to myself and go outside, because it's going to make everything better.

The physical act of sitting in the grass helps me get grounded. My focus shifts outward. I look right in front of me and see teeny things that you wouldn't ordinarily notice, like snails, tiny flowers, or insects moving around. I listen to the birdsong or the breeze in the tree branches. I sit in wordless contemplation; thoughts may come and go but I don't follow them. Sometimes I'll take pictures of my discoveries so I can share them with others on my social media feeds.

Occasionally I lead groups on early morning nature walks. We'll go to Audubon Park or by the Mississippi River and walk in silence. That's a really beautiful way to begin the day. Once or twice a week I will also walk around my neighborhood, just being present while I walk.

I like making tea, especially in the winter. I might take it outside with me and sip while I sit. I have particular cups I like, but no special rituals aside from slowing down to savor the tea. I have several flavors I love, like rose, Earl Grey, and Constant Comment. I'll choose the flavor based on my mood.

There have been times in the past when I've chosen poems or passages to read; I've also done morning pages (three pages of stream-of-consciousness, longhand writing), as Julia Cameron recommends in *The Artist's Way*. Sometimes I write; sometimes I receive messages from Spirit and write them down. I might also read aloud from my "soul statements" (which are like affirmations) that I have on my vision boards.

Some mornings I begin with yoga asanas. I have a few favorite poses to start the day, including tree pose, sun salutations, and half-moon pose. I like to roll my mat out on our back deck and greet the morning with some movement. Often the cats join me, curling between my legs.

I also have rituals that help me transition from free time into work time: I have an invocation that I say; I light palo santo and candles; I spray Florida water, which is scented with rose and orange blossom essence; and I might look at my vision boards. Sometimes I will also pull a card—I like the Angel Oracle cards—either just to see the message or to seek guidance about something particular.

Why a morning ritual is valuable to me

When I take time to meditate or sit outside, starting my morning slowly and with intention, it makes a real difference. It helps me connect with my essential self and sets the tone for the day. I have more compassion for others, the world, and the way I am in the world. For example, when I'm crossing the street, rather than seeing the traffic, I'll look at each person driving and think, "Oh, I hope you have a nice morning." I can come from a place of connection and compassion much more easily.

My suggestions for you

Often, we're living on autopilot. If we can sit in stillness and contemplation, it connects us to an expanded awareness and pure potentiality, and that spills over into what we do each day. It doesn't have to be long—just three to five minutes of being still is valuable. At the school where my husband teaches, they do a three-minute meditation with the students in homeroom each morning, and that really makes a positive difference in their attitudes and behavior.

It's very counterintuitive that doing less can be better for us, but it's true. Our culture is so action oriented and focused on achievement. Most people feel like it's not okay simply to be still. We worry that others will judge us for "not being productive," but it's important to take that time.

It's also important to pay attention to what's working for us. Sometimes I find myself feeling disengaged from the particular ritual I'm doing, trying to get through it just to cross it off the list, which doesn't serve me and misses the whole point of any ritual in the first place. That's why I switch up what I do, so

I can stay present. However, meditation and other rituals aren't meant to feel good all the time. There can be a level of discomfort, but that is good for us because beyond the discomfort is a deeper level of presence or connection. It's a fine line, and I search for it all the time.

My basic philosophy is, "Don't be mean to yourself about what you're doing or not doing." These days there are so many messages leading us to feel like what we're doing isn't enough, and that can generate so much shame. We're seeking, seeking, seeking some kind of recognition that we're living up to our fullest potential, when actually all is well and we are exactly on our path. Trying to improve our lives is wonderful, but only if we aren't beating ourselves up along the way. (I can make myself miserable with SIMU—stuff I made up—that I believe I'm "supposed to do," and that is not the way to happiness.)

It's vital to first treat yourself with love and kindness. Incorporate a ritual into your morning that feels good to you and serves you, then be relaxed about it and stay flexible. Keep listening to yourself to learn what works best for you.

TAKE A MOMENT

What appealed to you in this chapter?
What didn't appeal to you?
Did this chapter spark any ideas for you?

Being still, stream of conscious writing.
Finding connection to nature

2

Keri Wilt

KERI IS THE great-great-granddaughter of Frances Hodgson Burnett, author of *The Secret Garden*, *A Little Princess*, and many other beloved classics. She writes the blog *FHB and Me*, which features stories about her life inspired by quotes from Burnett's famous books. Keri is also working on her first book. She lives in the Texas Hill Country with her husband and two children.

"A recent "aha" realization that came out of my time in my journal was, 'If writing is my thing, why am I not writing to my kids? I need to connect with them through words, if this is the gift God gave me.' So I started texting them little things throughout the day and am exploring other ways to write a way into their hearts as they grow."

I have a fairly consistent morning ritual these days, but I'm always flexible. Different seasons in my life have called for different things. My ritual could be intricate or easy, depending on what is happening at that time—if I'm really busy with the kids, for example. There isn't one practice that has always worked; I do what's best for me for where I am at that moment.

Currently, I wake up and take my supplements first. I contracted a virus that caused Bell's palsy and am now very regimented about managing my health holistically. Next, I make a big cup of tea. I used to be very "tea snobbish" about it; I would buy only gourmet loose tea and brew it with the fancy strainer, but these days I prefer a simple premade bag of herbal or green tea. I especially enjoy the Traditional Medicinals brand with the fun quotes on the tabs. The warmth of the mug is so soothing first thing in the morning. I think I might like the experience of holding the warm mug just as much as drinking the tea, if not more!

I don't watch the news or read the paper in the morning; I don't want to start my day with negativity or allow myself to worry about things I can't control. It's funny because my great-great-grandmother was the exact same way. She is reported to have said, "I never read about ugly things that I cannot help. That is why I never read newspapers. They terrify me."

Most Monday through Friday mornings, after my supplements and tea, I sit with my journal. This process has evolved many times over the last five years. When I first began, I would read a daily devotional and write down the key verse. Later I would embellish it with colored markers and perhaps some simple drawings. I'm a "see it, say it, write it" kind of girl and need all three to be able to really let the messages sink in.

Journaling what I read helps me be quiet with it, think about it more deeply, and essentially process it better.

Today I have a somewhat longer process. First, I write the date at the top of the page and add three or four lines about the previous or current day—just super simple stuff to help me remember what was going on at that point in my life. Then I grab my phone. I have a folder on it called God Time, which contains about eleven devotional apps that I love. I'll read through about four or five of those at random, then write down what I call "head bob moments"—those lines that would make you bust out the highlighter if you were reading them in a book. I write them down freehand in my notebook how-ever I feel called to—big letters, small letters—leaving room in the margins. Then when I'm done, I read back over everything and pray through it, touching it one more time before I tackle my day.

I like to get up early before my family does because it's quiet, and I don't like to take time away from them. To keep myself whole, I gotta do me before I can do anybody else. Sometimes they'll also be up, but they are good about not disturbing me. However, if it's not completely peaceful in the house, or if I'm somewhere else, I'll use earphones to help me focus. I might play some soothing music or white noise. Quiet is important for me to be able to get into that centered space. Typically, my brain is always on the edge of overload, wander-ing and thinking about my to-do list. If you add the distraction of noise, I really can't focus.

My goal is to do my journaling before I do anything else. But sometimes the mornings are crazy and I have to com-plete my journaling at a coffee shop or in the pick-up line at school—wherever I can fit it in. I recently tried to write before journaling, and it was so hard. I just couldn't get my mind to connect. I wasn't in the right frame of mind.

Saturdays are the culmination of my journaling week. I love Saturdays! I get up, grab my Crayola Super Tips, and reread my entire week's journal entries. As I read, I color, highlight, and draw the big "aha" moments right on top of the journaled pages. This makes the important stuff stand out and shine brighter, making it easier to spot through all the clutter and messy handwriting. Some of what I write is fluff, and some of it is "*Yes ... this is important, Keri.*" This process helps me see the difference. If I don't color and highlight, the big things won't stand out in the sea of written words.

I'll begin to notice patterns, like the same word coming up over and over again. The devotionals I read are not connected at all—there's a real variety—so it stands out to me when they seem to be relaying a similar message. I underline or circle these, but typically, because I'm hardheaded, at first I won't see it; God has to really get my attention. After the second week of seeing the same thing over and over, I'm like, "Okay, okay, I hear you!"

A recent "aha" realization that came out of my time in my journal was, "If writing is my thing, why am I not writing to my kids? I need to connect with them through words, if this is the gift God gave me." So I started texting them little things throughout the day and am exploring other ways to write a way into their hearts as they grow.

Sundays are my "play in my Bible" days. I pick up my art journaling Bible, bought specifically for this purpose, close my eyes, and choose a page at random. If my family is up, I might hand it to my husband or child for them to pick a page. Then I sit somewhere quiet and read both pages in the spread. I used to try to color on both pages, but it became too time-consuming, so now I focus on one. When I find that head bob moment on the page that was meant just for me, I brainstorm about how I can draw this message or verse on the page.

For example, if the theme is about listening, perhaps I will color a picture of a bunny with oversized ears to remind myself to listen before I speak. I am not an artist, so I will search for pictures of bunnies on my phone; then, when I find one I like, I place the phone behind the page where I want the picture and simply trace and color it. What I draw isn't what I would call art. It's not meant to be perfect, it's just something I enjoy. The drawing and coloring feeds me in a totally different way than my weekday journaling, since I'm a word-driven person. It gets me outside of my box. It gives me a place to be creative each week. I do the marketing for the restaurant we own—designing posters and handling social media—but this is a different sort of creativity and I really have fun with it.

I first saw this type of Bible journaling on Instagram. It's called "illustrative faith." Like a tattoo, these pages tell the story of a time and a place in my life. It is a visual way for me to express what God was telling me on that page. And the cool thing is that I can read the same page of the Bible twelve different times in my life and I will get something totally different out of it each time.

I have other Bibles to read and study in the traditional way; this one isn't for that. This feels a little like a scrapbook. I can flip back through it and remember what was important on that day. With these pages, I'm celebrating my relationship with God. I realize that some people might be taken aback at the idea of writing in a Bible, but I believe a book is meant to be used. I write in and on all of the books I read, which makes it difficult to pass them on to others when I'm done! To me, the book is not the sacred item; it's the expression within that is sacred. And by engaging with it via my art, I have become connected through it and to it in a whole new way.

I can't wait for my kids to want to flip through the art journal Bible and my other journals and perhaps find something that they need at the time. But even if they don't do that, writing and drawing in these journals is still meaningful for me.

I also like to run-walk or do hot yoga. I try to do something active each day, but it's seasonal. Sometimes life gets in the way. When school is in session, there's a rhythm to the days and that makes exercise easier. The challenge is to figure out how to find our rhythm no matter what is happening around us! Regardless of what is going on, I try to have some grace with myself, my weight, my exercise habits, and my schedule.

Also, I don't think I could "do life" without my weekly ritual of coffee every Thursday morning with my girlfriends. Time with our friends is so important, and it doesn't happen unless we make it happen. As a writer, I spend a lot of time in my head. Having consistent time with others keeps me sane. My hour with my friends each week roots me, feeds my soul, and ties me together with the people who make me a better me.

Why a morning ritual is valuable to me

A morning ritual is important because it sets the tone and starts the day in a purposeful way. I'm centered, not rushed.

Journaling gives me time to think about what's going on and listen to God. The weekday journal is my playbook, like in football—it helps me to walk through every day, being intentional about the way I live and how I show love to those around me.

Taking the time each morning feels like a luxury some days, but really it's a toothbrushing moment: it's just as necessary for my well-being as brushing my teeth. When I exercise, eat right, and journal, I'm *such* a better me. It makes me clearheaded, focused, and able to walk better where He shines the light. I'm frazzled if one of those is off.

Most people let life happen to them instead of being purposeful. We have to clear out the clutter to have the space in our days to see what our purpose is, then let it in. Journaling is my meditation. It has set me on my current path of writing my blog and book, which has been exhilarating and rewarding.

When I started journaling about five years ago, I was so busy and overwhelmed with life. I started with fifteen minutes, then thirty; now I'll sometimes spend an hour if I have it. It was through those initial moments of silence with my journal that I began to wake up and crave more of the space, clarity, and direction that I was getting during that time. I had been doing a million different things—work, volunteering, parenting—and through my journal, I started hearing the call to clear my plate. I felt a longing to *not* be committed to everyone else *but* me. I was doing too much and I needed a total teardown of my life.

Now I feel so free! I have the time and can finally do what I'm called to do, which is write. I always had "writing a book" on my bucket list, but hadn't written a word since college. Then, two years ago, I took a class on a whim about how to write a story at Lucky Star Art Camp. In class, as I wrote about my great-great-grandmother Frances Hodgson Burnett, I was overwhelmed by a feeling of, "Oh, I remember this ... and I really like it!"

It was there that the seeds of writing were replanted in my heart, and the idea of a blog began to grow. I figured a blog would force me to write on a regular basis; I wasn't confident enough in my writing yet to jump straight into working on a book. I spent a lot of time that next year brainstorming and gathering ideas. Then, while I was reading *The Secret Garden* at night, God began showing me through my journaling the next morning almost the exact quote or theme that I had read the night before. For the first time, I began to realize how life-changing and inspiring FHB's words were and how, if combined with my real life stories, they might have an impact and help others to live a life in full bloom.

I started my blog, *FHB and Me*, in June of 2016. Recently, I've gotten to a comfortable place with it and have started work on my first book, *Life Lessons from "The Secret Garden."* I hadn't thought that I was "ready" or "good enough" to start writing it in earnest. Then one morning I was working in my garden, listening to Laura Casey's *Make It Happen* on audiotape, and she said, "Life is too short to not do the thing God has called you to do." I turned off the water, walked inside, and told my husband, "I'm doing this!" Laura is right: life is too short ... so I am going for it. It's all very exciting and scary at the same time. And to think, this whole writing adventure began because I gave myself the space, through my morning rituals, to find my purpose.

My suggestions for you

Be flexible. Change is good. What works today may not work in a year or even a month. If it's not working anymore, switch it up and find a new groove. In the beginning I was too regimented about the way I journaled. Then one day I accidently left my car sunroof open and it rained directly into the bag containing my notebook. I had been using washable markers to write down the verses, which were now running down the pages. My journal was ruined. I was devastated by the loss. Then my husband said, in his matter-of-fact way, "Well, Keri, I guess it's time to do something new." I thought, "Huh, okay." He was right, and switching it up was just what I needed to connect even deeper. Today, I'm less attached to the final product.

Understand that life can and will get in the way of the things you have planned, so try not to stress about getting thrown a little off balance. The important thing is to learn how to get back on track after the storm comes, and to be kind to yourself during that process.

Explore what others are doing that is helpful and uplifting for them, and find a way to make it your own. Then look at your day and honestly see if you're utilizing your moments correctly. I put a tracker on my phone to limit the time I spend on social media. It was eye-opening—you think you're on there for just a few minutes and an hour goes by. You think, "What could I have done with that hour?"

And try to wake up a little earlier each day. Getting up thirty minutes earlier will not wreck your day, but the power it has to make your day—and you—better is worth it. Starting each day hurried and crazy is not the way to live.

Start small, but just start … anything. For example, just sit and have tea alone every morning. Make space for yourself so you can start hearing what you're meant to do and can begin to grow toward living your life in full bloom.

Take a Moment

What appealed to you in this chapter?
What didn't appeal to you?
Did this chapter spark any ideas for you?

3

Cynthia Morris

CYNTHIA IS AN author, artist, speaker, creativity coach, and book coach. With her Capture the Wow workshops, she leads creative adventures in inspirational destinations like Paris. She also offers online workshops and travels the world giving presentations. She lives with her husband in Denver, Colorado.

"I tell my clients to make time for creative projects, as creativity feeds you and enhances your vitality, whether you're an artist or not. ... [When I don't have early appointments] I like to go into my art studio and start the day there. Art is so fun and playful."

I started my morning ritual in 2013 with a seated meditation practice. To keep myself on track, I made just one decision—I would meditate every day—rather than choosing each day whether or not I would do it. I was participating in The Good Life Project at the time and was supported by a community of people who were looking to create a more balanced life, which really helped me. One of my close friends teaches meditation, so it also helped to have someone I knew to model that life for me.

I meditated first thing, before my mind started going too much, so I was better able to focus. I used the Insight Timer app for its tracking and accountability functions. I like to track myself; it motivates me. I started with ten minutes each morning, and built up to twenty.

Earlier this year I stopped meditating for several reasons. One was that my boyfriend (now husband) moved in. Instead of meditating, I would spend the first part of the morning with him, snuggling and talking. Meditation had served as a gentle onboarding to the day for me. Now this time with him did the same thing and was really beneficial to our relationship. It helped us feel connected all day.

Another reason was that I began to wonder, "Why am I doing this? Is it in order to feel good—or to look good?" I had been featured in *Yoga Journal Magazine* for my practice, and also was using the social accountability feature on the Insight Timer app, and it started to feel less genuine. It seemed to be less about what I wanted to do and more about how it made me appear to others.

Now I'm coming back to meditation because I miss it. My goal is to meditate every day, starting at ten minutes again. I have a short fuse and can get angry easily; this morning I got upset about the traffic. I did some deep breathing and the anger went away. It was interesting to notice how my thoughts triggered the angry reaction. I realized that meditation helps me to be aware of my thoughts and handle them before I react.

Meditating has a very positive effect, but it can be subtle. At first, the benefits aren't obvious; then you realize, "Oh, I'm calmer and less short-tempered when I do it regularly!"

Because I *want* to start meditating again, it will feel good to me. I will feel integrity in it because I'm doing what I want to do *and* what I said I would. It's both external and internal.

There are other aspects to my morning ritual. I like to draw an angel card and a tarot card and ask, "What do I need? What will help me today?" That can provide some useful messages.

I also love to have coffee in the morning—it's my big treat. I try to enjoy it mindfully, without checking my email. I feel better when I don't go to the computer right away. When I was first starting my business, I would think, "It's 6:00 a.m.; I have to get to work." Now I feel like, "It's 6:00 a.m.; I can relax and enjoy this time for myself."

I might journal occasionally, although I don't write as much as I used to. I have stacks of journals from previous years when I would do morning pages every day. I read *The Artist's Way* by Julia Cameron and did her program in 1994–95; it totally changed my life. I recommend that book to everyone. It's an excellent tool for finding out what lights you up. When I reread it five years ago, I was amazed to see how much it had informed my coaching philosophy. For instance, I tell my clients to make time for creative projects, as creativity feeds you and enhances your vitality, whether you're an artist or not.

When I have appointments, I will go straight to work after I finish my coffee. But when I don't, I like to go into my art studio and start the day there. Art is so fun and playful, and I love my studio. I have a table by the window and a little desk. It's marvelous to have this dedicated space now.

I haven't always been an artist. I got into art around 1996 when I was working in a used bookstore and discovered Frederick Franck (*The Zen of Seeing*). He used drawing as meditation—as a way of seeing something, communing with it, and drawing from that connectedness. At the time I couldn't sit still to meditate, so I tried that instead and loved it. I began to sketch a lot. I wasn't great but I enjoyed it.

In 2005 I started leading creativity workshops in France, where I showed people how to use sketchbooks to record their experiences, both in travel and life. I was still mainly writing and just doing art on the side. Once I published my novel, *Chasing Sylvia Beach*, in 2012, it freed me to focus more on art.

As I reincorporate meditation into my morning ritual, I'm looking for ways to enhance the experience and make it more meaningful. Recently, I heard Hal Elrod on a podcast, and I started reading his book *The Miracle Morning*. He talks about the value of getting up very early—like 4:00 a.m.—and doing a structured set of practices to enhance your productivity. I naturally wake up early, so I don't need his advice on that, but I like the idea of having more structure to my morning. I also like how he gives you something to focus on, with questions to answer about life goals and what's important to you. I won't be following all of his suggestions—it's a little too rigid for me—but I'm interested in incorporating that type of focus into my meditation to make it more robust and practical.

Why a morning ritual is valuable to me

It's beneficial to be mindful in the morning. Morning rituals provide space for self-connection and self-knowledge. It's a compelling concept to me that how I start the day determines the quality of my day and my life. As I mentioned before, I find that when I meditate in the morning, I'm calmer and less short-tempered, which definitely improves my quality of life!

When we do a morning ritual, we're putting ourselves first. We're focusing on our relationship with ourselves, so we know what we want and then are able to create it.

It's very powerful to envision what sort of life we want. Years ago, I read a book called *The Lotus and the Lily*, which led me through a process for connecting to my sacred self and outlining my dreams. The author's method of making a wish list is very rich and interesting; it ensures that the desires are coming from our soul rather than our ego. I had the best year ever after I did that. I want to do it again and see if it was just a coincidence, or if it was the power of that process and the intentions I set!

My suggestions for you

Women—especially mothers—need a good morning ritual. You can feel responsible for the whole family. It's tough to fit your own stuff in. But it's necessary. A ritual helps you identify what you want so you can achieve it. However, it doesn't have to be first thing in the morning if that doesn't work for you. If you're a mom, you may not be able to do anything for yourself in the morning. Pick another time if you need to, and make it your time.

To create the ritual that works best for you, look at all the choices out there and see what resonates. What appeals to you? What sparks a "that sounds interesting" feeling? Then experiment. Just try something for two weeks. Be aware of the impact of what you're doing—what do you notice is different?—so you're connecting to the impact of the practice and not just the practice itself. For example, you might notice, "I'm calmer when I meditate." So you enjoy being calmer, and the meditation is just a path to get there.

Then adapt as needed. Make it work for your circumstances—and your body. A big thing I recommend to clients is to let the body lead. I learned that from experiencing jet lag. Your body is really in charge—it was a powerful realization for me. If we don't have energy or are ill, we can't do what we want; but our mind tends to drag our body around. Pay attention to how your body responds to what you try. For instance, if you're meditating, it might not feel good to sit on the floor, so you could sit on a chair instead.

If you like to move, maybe you'd rather go for a walk first thing in the morning. It's such a basic human need—your body wants to move; it was designed for that. And exercise can really benefit us mentally as well as physically. Recently, for about four days in a row, I woke up at 5:00 a.m. and went for a walk. It was wonderful. The air was cool and fresh, and I loved the feeling of being out there with no one else around—like I was getting the world before others did.

I think journaling can be a useful practice, especially if you use some prompts. Questions are helpful. I love morning pages and highly recommend them, but I can't write randomly for three pages anymore—I need something to think about, like,

"What do I want for myself?" If you're stuck and not getting answers, I recommend trying a different question.

I have a great writing prompt I give people so they can get to the truth: "What I really want to say is ..." In your journal you can be totally honest. Women especially have a hard time being honest about how we feel or what we need; we don't want to hurt or upset anyone. A journal can be a safe, private place for you to let go and say whatever you want.

If you can't keep your ritual going, it's okay. Don't beat yourself up. Expect it. Be curious about what got you off track. It's often an external circumstance, but it may also be internal. I wasn't sad about stopping meditation, because I wasn't doing it for me anymore. Quitting it at the time gave me a sense of freedom. Now I'm coming back to it because I want to, but also thinking about what I might tweak so that I'm more actively engaged and growing. It's less important to stick with a ritual than it is to be flexible. Don't feel like you have to keep doing something if it no longer helps you. Adapt it to your changing needs.

TAKE A MOMENT

What appealed to you in this chapter?
What didn't appeal to you?
Did this chapter spark any ideas for you?

4

Tonya Lewis Lee

TONYA IS AN author, filmmaker, entrepreneur, and health and wellness advocate. She runs the website HealthyYouNow. com and is a founder of Movita Organics, which produces an organic women's multivitamin. She lives in New York City with her two children and her husband, Spike Lee.

"Before I leave home, I will spray some essential orange oil in my hands, rub them together, and breathe it in for about thirty seconds. It's like a quick meditation before I head out. This enhances my creativity and gets me ready for the day."

I joke with my friends about how we start the day in chaos, so I think morning rituals are very important.

I don't meditate formally, but I like to take some time in bed before I get up. I will lie there and mentally go through a checklist so I'm mindful of what needs to happen that day. This helps me feel organized before I even get out of bed.

I go through phases where I wake up early, like around 6:00 a.m., and go to the gym first thing. I love to get up as the sun is rising, go exercise, and then come out just as people are beginning to mill around—it's like I've gotten a jump on the day. That's the best feeling.

I tend to wake up at 7:00 a.m. normally, but when I get in that phase of waking up at 6:00, that's when my days go great. Since the gym is right across the street from my house, I really should go every day, but I don't. And I can beat myself up when I don't. I feel like it should be easy for me, but it's hard to get up early—it just is—and I can't do it every day.

The best is in the spring, when the sun's coming up earlier, the weather is warmer, and I'm inspired. In the winter when it's dark and cold, it's harder. But we have to respect the natural cycles of our bodies. We're meant to sort of hibernate in winter; the body instinctively wants to rest then.

My husband is an early riser—he gets up at 5:00 a.m. no matter what. I prefer to wake up on my own. It's not cool when he wakes me up, which he knows, so he's good about being quiet. I wish I could get up that early, though. It's amazing how he does it no matter where in the world he is or what's going on.

Ideally I like to wake up at 6:00 a.m., get to the gym at 6:15, and be home by 7:00. Then I can have coffee and relax.

I enjoy doing *The New York Times'* crossword puzzle while I drink my coffee. It wakes my brain up. On those mornings when I've exercised both my body and my brain, I'm really good to go.

In the morning I'll also make a smoothie. I have this amazing recipe with blueberry, spinach, cocoa powder, protein powder, and coconut water. It's so good. I feel like I'm feeding both my body and my brain when I drink it. Afterward I feel just right: nourished but not too full. When I don't have my smoothie—for instance, when I'm traveling—I'm a little off all day.

So if I have my coffee and my smoothie, I'm happy. If I've worked out as well, then I feel like I'm in charge; I'm taking care of business, and there's no stopping me.

Before I leave home, I will spray some essential orange oil in my hands, rub them together, and breathe it in for about thirty seconds. It's like a quick meditation before I head out. This enhances my creativity and gets me ready for the day. Sometimes, when it's hectic, all I have is that little bit of time.

Why a morning ritual is valuable to me

It's important to take a moment before the busy day starts. I love my bed. After I wake up, I like to stay there for a bit so I'm not rushing into things—those days are never good. I set an alarm but tend to wake up before it, so I'll stay in bed until it goes off. Then it seems as if I'm getting some extra time, and I get up mentally prepared for the day.

Exercising first thing gives me an edge; I feel like I've got a jumpstart on everyone else. In addition to the physical benefits and that endorphin rush, I'm calmer and more focused. Exercising makes me feel good both mentally and physically.

Also, I like knowing that I've done something for myself. That makes me feel good too.

My suggestions for you

When you wake up, give yourself a few minutes to lie in bed and breathe; don't do anything else. I know it's hard, especially if you have little kids. That's a whole different ball game. My children are grown now, but I've been there—when your kids come in and wake you up and you don't have your own time. If that's your life right now, just try another part of the day. I believe you can create time for yourself no matter what. Just close your eyes and breathe—even if it's only five minutes and you have to lock yourself in the bathroom. It's even more crucial to carve out some alone time when you're in that chaotic period of life.

I also think exercising in the morning is a great way to start the day. But it's not for everyone, and like I said, even though I love to, I can't work out every morning. It's important that we respect ourselves and our needs. Sometimes you're just tired, and you should listen to your body and rest if you need to.

Overall, I think the most vital thing is taking quiet time for yourself. I know it because I've lived it. That's when you hear your own voice and find your own truth. That's how you figure out what you're supposed to do. My philosophy of life is that we are all here for a purpose; everyone has something valuable to contribute. Sometimes that can get lost because we're reacting to everything else in life, doing what others want us to do rather than what we want. This is especially true for women. So whether it's in the morning or at another time, be sure to make some space to hear yourself each day.

Take a Moment

What appealed to you in this chapter?
What didn't appeal to you?
Did this chapter spark any ideas for you?

5

Anna Kunnecke

ANNA IS A life coach who helps women "declare dominion over their gorgeous lives," learn how to set boundaries, and reclaim their personal power. She lives in Canada with her husband and their five children.

"My morning ritual gives me a chance to clear my mind of everyone else's priorities for me. ... I'm not being shaped by the forces around me; I'm shaping my world from my mind and heart."

I find most people's morning rituals super intimidating. I'm not a morning person at all. I'm never going to do that hard-core stuff like get up at 4:00 a.m. and work out. About seventy-four million times in my life I've tried to be the person who gets up at 4:00, but I'm the absolute worst in the morning. I'm not myself until 11:00 a.m. I can stay up until 3:00 a.m., no problem, but I can't wake up super early. And you're not supposed to admit that, right? But it's the truth for me.

My mornings have changed dramatically in the last several months. Before, I was a single mom raising a daughter in Portland, Oregon. Now I'm married with five kids, and my husband and I both work from home. Some of what I get to do now is the result of life giving me gifts rather than my own actions. I'm very lucky.

These days, my husband gets up before me to get the kids ready for school. He's a morning person who is wiped out after dinner, so he doesn't mind being up early. I do all the prep the night before—that's when my ritual actually starts. I lay out clothes, make lunches, and get everything ready. All he has to do is grab things and go.

I get to sleep in most mornings. Sometimes my husband will even make a cup of tea and leave it for me before he goes, which is really sweet. When I wake up, I pull out my journal and do morning pages (from *The Artist's Way* by Julia Cameron). Those are the very best things I can do for my soul and mind. I just dump everything and clear it all out. I will write down concerns, dreams, whatever's in my head.

Then I pull a couple of tarot cards—I like the Wild Unknown deck—to see what message they might have for me. Next, I get dressed. I wear real clothes every day; it's important to me to dress like my best self even though I'm working at home.

After that, I update my Daily Compass, a tool I created, which is a map of my day. I plug in appointments, block out work time, and plan my entire day in advance. Then I identify my top priority for the day—the one thing I must get done. I print out the Daily Compass and often put a sticker to make it pretty. I try to add beauty wherever I can!

Sometimes I'll do a little energy hygiene if I need it; I will sit quietly, connect with my energy, and set boundaries. And I always make my bed! Such a small detail, but it really helps me feel like I'm on top of things.

This has been my morning ritual for the last few months. Before that, when I was a solo parent, it looked very different! I would get up early, get my daughter ready, put on casual or workout clothes, and walk her to school. I would take a circuitous route and power walk for about twenty to thirty minutes on the way back, coming home sweaty and with my mind clear.

Then I would shower and dress in real clothes, make tea, and do my morning pages and Daily Compass. I would still do my ritual, but only after I had taken care of my mom responsibilities. I wasn't able to get up and do my stuff ahead of time, so I fit it in afterward. If I had a client call early, I would condense everything into a shorter time frame.

There are some practices I've tried that don't work for me. For example, I've attempted multiple times to write first thing in the morning, as I've read that many writers do that, but it only led to guilt, shame, and self-loathing. Now I commit to writing ten minutes a day, and squeeze it in whenever I can. I know Elizabeth Gilbert recommends thirty minutes a day, but if I say thirty minutes, then I just won't do it at all. It seems like too much. However, I will often keep going after I've finished the initial ten minutes.

For work projects, I block out longer chunks, and every now and then I'll go to a hotel for two or three days and write around the clock. No distractions! I have to be out of my home to write for larger projects, away from all the obligations.

I've tried to meditate, but I do it poorly and irregularly. I don't dislike it, but morning pages, tarot cards, and walking serve as my meditation. They yield more peace of mind for me than meditation does.

Why a morning ritual is valuable to me

My morning ritual gives me a chance to clear my mind of everyone else's priorities for me. Email, Facebook, Instagram, the news: it all wants me to do something. When I set my priorities first before I look at that stuff, I'm steering my course. I'm not being shaped by the forces around me. I'm shaping my world from my mind and heart.

My suggestions for you

The most important thing for me, and what I recommend to anyone starting out, is to choose the top priority for the day. The other stuff is beautiful and wonderful, but it's not vital. Your daily priority is the engine that drives everything. The rest is just the shiny exterior and plush upholstery. Especially if you're a parent, you can get pulled in all directions each day and never get done what you need to. Setting a daily priority helps keep you on track.

You don't have to do it in bed with tea, either. That's lovely but not necessary. I used to live in Tokyo and had to get up early for work, so I would jot my daily priority down in my Day-Timer while I was on the subway.

Life is messy and complicated and we're all just doing the best we can. If you are starting to implement a ritual, keep it simple and tag it onto something you already do, like making coffee or commuting to work.

Also, add only one thing at a time. We sabotage ourselves by thinking, "Yes! I'm going to get up at 4:00 every morning and do this, this, and this!" When you read about rituals that others have created over time, it can be intimidating. Even a twenty-minute ritual can seem overwhelming at first.

Start with just one thirty-second or sixty-second action. Doing a sixty-second ritual every day will give you a lot more bang for your buck than doing a three-hour ritual once or twice. Then, as you implement that and do it for about three months, you'll feel the results of the habit, and it will be easier to add more if you want to.

TAKE A MOMENT

What appealed to you in this chapter?
What didn't appeal to you?
Did this chapter spark any ideas for you?

6

Tracy Verdugo

Tracy is a "prolific painter and inspiration instigator" and author of the book *Paint Mojo*. She travels the world teaching creativity workshops, reminding her students of the wonder that already resides within them. She lives in Australia with her husband. They have two daughters in their twenties.

"Since starting my morning ritual, I feel more centered and definitely less anxious. … meditating really helps. It makes me feel connected to Spirit. I also feel stronger and more able to speak my truth without worrying about what others will say."

I've just been getting into having a morning ritual over the last year or two. I'm a work in progress; every day is a different day. From my perspective, it's important to acknowledge that rituals are wonderful and helpful, but they won't make your life perfect. It's not like I'll wake up one morning, and I'll be this Zen-like creature, and every day from here on out is perfect. You have to allow for life, and life is messy.

I have had health issues over the last few years. That has caused me to really look at how I was moving through the world, and I realized I was never switching off. Now I try to take breaks throughout the day. I also cut down on work obligations by scheduling fewer workshops and trips. I was doing twenty a year, all around the world. I get very excited when I'm planning things, and don't always realize the reality of booking all those events two years out. So now instead of acting right away, I'll think about it first—pause for a day or so and then come back to it.

I also took seven months completely off this year, which was big. That gave me a chance to regroup and process some of the amazing experiences I've had in the last five years on all those trips. I was able to spend time in my studio and experiment and play. It's been a beautiful time and very restorative.

My morning ritual starts with gratitude before I even get out of bed. After I wake up, I will say thank you. I think it's really important to do that. I used to wake up and think about work right away, which was stressful. Now I've created this habit of being thankful first thing instead, and it's a much better way to start my day.

Next, I will meditate. My husband has been meditating for about thirty years. He does so first thing every morning. We actually have a dedicated meditation tower that my husband built; you can only access it by a bridge from our bedroom. I've always resisted, but a couple of years ago I decided to stop saying, "Oh, I can't meditate." I'm still not great at it, but I go in there and I sit.

Several years back my mum sent me a pair of little orange sandals that were mine when I was two years old. I have them on the altar in the meditation room, and I will pick them up, hold them, light some sage, and put a protective barrier of love and light around them and the child I was. It's a way to reconnect with her and let her know she is loved.

Also on my altar is a little statue of the Virgin Mary from Mexico. In 2008 we took our girls out of school and did a big trip around the U.S. and Mexico. We visited this little beach village near Oaxaca, and we saw all these people coming in with a statue of the Virgin Mary, but she looked different. We found out that the people were coming from a tiny village way up in the mountains called Juqulila, and back in the 1500s this statue of Mary was brought there and put into the church. Years later there was a huge fire, and everything burned except her. However, her skin had blackened—so now she looked like the indigenous people of the area! She became very special to them, and every year people come from all over on pilgrimage to see her and ask for miracles. We just happened to be there during the pilgrimage.

So we have a little Virgin Mary statue from there on our altar, and I speak to her every morning. It's usually about self-worth, issues going on that I need to deal with, and how to be easier on myself.

Sometimes after that, I will stay and meditate for about fifteen to twenty minutes more—it depends on how much chatter is in my head that day. I play a little game with myself: how long can I stop a thought from coming? Usually it's just about thirty seconds! Then a thought comes in … I'll watch it, I'll let it go, and another comes.

I like this practice because it allows us to begin again in every moment. I have an exercise I do in my art classes if students are getting overwhelmed. I'll have them paint "Begin Again" in white ink in the center of this painting they've been working on for days, then cover it with layers of various materials. It's to remind them to give themselves permission to start over.

We can always begin again, no matter what. We're okay in all of our confusion and complexity. So with meditation, even if it's just thirty seconds of quiet and stillness, that's okay. We can begin again after that.

In the meditation room we also have books, and I might open one to a random page and see what message it has for me. We also have Sacred Path meditation cards, and I may pick one to see what it says.

Afterward, a very important part of my morning is to have some freshly squeezed juice. My favorite is to combine carrot, apple, orange, ginger, and fresh turmeric. The day's not starting out right if I don't put that goodness in me. I also will drink some bicarbonate of soda and lemon in hot water for the alkalizing effect. Then I get to have my coffee!

During summer, we might go out and do some stand-up paddleboarding in the morning. It gives such a better direction for the day. I love getting outside and putting my feet on the earth—it's a great way of grounding myself. But in winter I tend to hibernate. On those mornings I'm more likely to curl up on the couch with my coffee and iPad!

I think it's also important to do mini rituals throughout the day. I set an alarm every hour and a half when I'm at my computer, and I'll get up and move. I might do a little dance party, or go outside and lie on the grass and get some sun, or do some stretches.

Painting is also a form of meditation for me. It's a mindfulness practice. I recently heard that the state we go into when we're meditating is the same as being in flow when we're making art, so those activities do have a similar effect on your brain. It helps me to let go of distractions and "busy-ness." It's extremely beneficial. Painting provides the space to let go of what's worrying us and to drop the chatter for a while.

I also have rituals I do in the studio. If I'm feeling scattered, I will straighten up first. If my mind is messy, it helps to clean up my physical space. I also may light incense, put on music, or dance a little before I get started.

Why a morning ritual is valuable to me

Lately I've been listening to podcasts about how being so connected with our devices all the time makes us scattered and unfocused. We need to come back to mindfulness, and a morning ritual helps with that. My morning practice also helps me show up in the best way I can every day.

Since starting my morning ritual, I feel more centered and definitely less anxious. I had twenty-five years of anxiety and panic attacks off and on; I've been working on that over the last ten years and haven't had symptoms in that time, so I was already improving, but meditating really helps. It makes me feel connected to Spirit.

I also feel stronger and more able to speak my truth without worrying about what others will say. I'm able to say no without being afraid that people won't like me. As a kid I was always so concerned about what others would say—I would rehearse conversations in my head—and I carried that into adulthood. Now I'm finally doing it a lot less. It only took me fifty-two years to get here! I have a stronger sense of self and am more at ease in my own skin.

My suggestions for you

I think the concept of counting your blessings is so important. To say thank you for what you have and the fact that you woke up that morning—that's a great way to start your day. Do what you can to cultivate that habit of gratitude first thing in the morning and then go from there. Sometimes you won't feel like it. You might be tired or wake up in a bad mood. But if you're able to catch yourself and do it anyway, you'll realize, "Hey, it shifted my mood."

Then the day flows more easily. It doesn't avalanche from bad mood to argument to mishap. You know how that can happen—something goes wrong first thing and it seems like bad stuff just keeps happening. If you have a centering ritual in the morning, especially if it's around gratitude or self-acceptance, your day can switch right there. It will then unfold in a different, better way. You'll attract positive rather than negative things.

TAKE A MOMENT

What appealed to you in this chapter?
What didn't appeal to you?
Did this chapter spark any ideas for you?

7

Christie Federico

CHRISTIE LIVES IN New Jersey and is a life coach who focuses on helping millennials and others lead authentic lives. She has a master's degree in mental health counseling, has worked as a therapist, and is certified by the Life Coach Training Institute.

"Lately I've been talking on the phone to my friend in the mornings. It's very important to me to feel connected, and since I live alone, this is an excellent way to do that. Talking with her gives me a happy and fulfilled feeling."

My morning ritual focuses on self-care. My schedule is currently all over the place, so each morning is different in terms of how much time I have. I vary what I do, depending on how

I feel that day and what I need—do I need to be uplifted or calmed down, or do I just need to maintain a good mood? I follow my intuition as to how to feel the best emotionally and physically, and how to have the clearest mind.

Regardless of what else I do, I always brush my teeth and shower first; I want to feel clean and confident. I also make decisions about how I wear my hair and what clothes I choose based on that goal of feeling my best.

I naturally wake up between 7:00 and 8:00 a.m., but some mornings I set an alarm for earlier. One day a week I work in New York City, so I get up early to commute. I also work part-time at a university. The hours there vary, so sometimes I need to get up early for that as well.

The rest of the time I work from home as a life coach. My goal is to help people of all ages with a motivational, solution-focused, holistic approach. As a millennial who has struggled with authenticity throughout my life, I understand how hard it can be. It's important to be your true self in all aspects—career as well as personal and romantic relationships—but that can be difficult in today's world. With social media, we can easily get caught up in others' lives, feel like we're not good enough, and be scared of being judged.

Before I begin work, I'll do something for myself. Lately I've been talking on the phone to my friend in the mornings. It's very important to me to feel connected, and since I live alone, this is an excellent way to do that. Talking with her gives me a happy and fulfilled feeling, whether it's through casual conversation, deep discussion, or just laughing together. I've been doing that on and off for about a year. I really enjoy starting my day this way because it puts me in a good mood, which lasts all day long.

Also, music is very important to me, so I often start the day by listening to something I love. I've done this for most of my life. A lot of times I like to put on disco because it's really upbeat. Sometimes I listen to something mellow; it just depends on how I'm feeling in the moment. Music is a powerful way to affect our mood.

I like to have a healthy breakfast to nourish my body, like a smoothie or oatmeal. In order to feel my best and be able to listen to my intuition, I need a clear mind, and I believe in the power of food to help give me that mental clarity. I try to drink water or tea first thing as well, but I'm not always consistent. I take a variety of supplements, depending on what I'll be eating the rest of the day and if I need extra energy.

When I have time, I might do a few yoga poses or lift free weights, especially if I know I won't be very active that day.

I have tried to meditate, and I wish I could be that person; I've read about it and tried some apps, but it just doesn't work for me currently. I've also tried to be the kind of person who could get up early and run or do a full hour of yoga before starting my day, but that's just not me.

Why a morning ritual is valuable to me

Self-care helps me access my intuition and gives me clarity. Connecting with a friend, taking supplements, eating a healthy breakfast, wearing clothes that make me feel confident—these are all ways that I take care of myself. When I clear out toxicity, whether it's emotional or physical, it makes it easier to think about what's important to me and then act on it.

My suggestions for you

Start simple. When you're just beginning, it's helpful to start small if you want to be consistent.

Create your ritual according to what you feel in your gut will bring you confidence and clarity. What makes you feel good? What will help you put your best foot forward?

Also, try incorporating music you love into your morning. I know some people say they're not really into it, but I strongly believe in the power of music to heal and to improve our mood. I encourage you to give it a try. Put something on and see how it affects you. Music can help motivate you, give you more energy, or make you feel calmer. Experiment with different types and see what results you can get. I bet you will really enjoy it!

TAKE A MOMENT

What appealed to you in this chapter?
What didn't appeal to you?
Did this chapter spark any ideas for you?

8

Sonia Sommer

S ONIA IS A Master Healer who "bridges the gap between
woo woo and doable." She combines physical, mental,
and spiritual tools to help people feel their best in all of those
aspects. She lives with her family in Sun Valley, Idaho.

*"You're already doing a ritual of some sort.
The question is, is there any life force in it? …
Remember the grace, beauty, and magic that live
in you. It's like your radio … set yourself on the
highest possible frequency for the day."*

I don't do the same thing every morning. I have practices that
I rotate around, depending on the day. Some mornings I have
five minutes, some an hour. I'm not too attached to any particular ritual. I just choose whatever works best at that time.

When I wake up, I take a look at what I dreamed about, then I gauge my frame of mind. I practice nonattachment to my feelings and just observe without judging. For example, if I wake up grumpy, I'll view that with interest. Then I will consciously shift into a mindset of gratitude and appreciation.

If I wake up tired, I will feel into what I need to do to replenish my energy. I'll choose from a list of rituals—activities that take care of body, brain, and soul. These include sitting in stillness, connecting with Spirit, drinking green juice and bone stock, and getting exercise—I like to run.

If I'm feeling sluggish, I will do some oil pulling, which helps remove toxins from the body. I swish a tablespoon or so of organic coconut oil or olive oil in my mouth for about fifteen minutes, then spit it out in the trash and rinse with sea-salt water. Then I'll brush my teeth with baking soda, and follow up by drinking a glass of warm water with lemon in it.

Most mornings I like to go outside first thing and feel the sun on my face. I might make a cup of tea or coffee beforehand and take that with me. I sit on the ground and remember that I'm a part of nature; it's a whole different perspective with which to greet the world. I recognize that I'm a soul having an experience and there's something bigger than me. It's a morning reset.

Sitting in stillness is something I often do. I like to sit for about an hour if I have time. I use a variety of techniques to get into the right mental space. I did Chi Kung for about a decade, and that really helped me. It tuned my system and made it easier for me to access that state. I'll get quiet in my mind, and after a bit my thoughts will almost disappear altogether. This brings me to a deep, unshakeable ground from which to live my life. Sometimes I'm not so successful, but that's okay. It's important just to sit and stay with it. [Author's note: this spelling of Chi Kung is Sonia's preference; it can also be spelled Qi Gong.]

Why a morning ritual is valuable to me

The world needs help right now. Those of us who are called need to hone ourselves to be our best selves so that we can help people return to their true nature and restore harmony with each other and our home here on earth. It's an urgent calling, and it requires me to reclaim my spot in nature every day so I can feel what's happening and what's needed.

We're all built for something, and we need to do what we're made to do. It's our responsibility as the keepers of the earth. My morning ritual helps me see clearly what to do.

My suggestions for you

We each start our day in a certain way, whether we're intentional about it or not. For some people, it's watching the news, which can be a fearful way to start. For others, it's something like sitting outside and remembering that we're more than our body. We're also a soul, which is much more magical and nourishing.

So you're already doing a ritual of some sort. The question is, is there any life force in it, or are you going through the motions? If you wake up stressed, make coffee, and gulp it down while you check emails, that can be lifeless. It doesn't feed your soul.

Remember the grace, beauty, and magic that live in you. It's like your radio, where you have preset stations: set yourself on the highest possible frequency for the day. There's a level of sacred reality where synchronicity is the norm, where wisdom, insight, and exactly what you need show up when you need it. Tune into that each day and your whole life will change.

Even when times are tough, how do you find the good? Keep trying to raise your perspective. Say, "I may feel like crap, but I'm alive!" Keep shifting up. When you're down, you feel heavy and slow because you are in that lower vibration. Shift up to feel lighter and easier.

If you want to experience magic in your life, it's critical to retrain your brain. Focus on accessing your right brain, where the magic happens. It's usually easier to access it in deep nature. That environment facilitates more mystical experiences. Creative activities like dance, art, and music are also wonderful right brain activators. Anything you loved to do as a kid, start doing it again and you will begin coming back to life.

Play around with making every moment of the day a sacred ritual. Live wholeheartedly. If you make life really fun and interesting, you line yourself up with the synchronistic ease that's always there. These moments can be about connecting with someone, whether it's someone you know or the checkout person at the grocery store, or about following your instincts. For example, I generally walk to and from work. The other day I was walking past a hill and I thought, "I really want to climb that hill." I was running a little late and needed to get home, but I followed my instincts and climbed it. When I got to the top and sat down, I had a beautiful experience and received some deep wisdom and guidance for my life. If you're present and aware, you open yourself up to those types of occurrences.

If you'd like to meditate but you have trouble sitting still, try doing some sort of physical action, like Chi Kung, tai chi, or yoga. Those help align body, mind, and spirit.

Be open to change. Some rituals work well for a period of time, and then they just don't fit in your life anymore. I had some seemingly great rituals that stopped working well. For instance, I used to do a particular form of Chi Kung. I would practice it three to four hours a day and I really loved it. Then I realized I was getting disconnected from my real life. I would tell my family not to bother me, I had to do my Chi Kung! So while something can be helpful at first, you can take it too far. Just be aware of how you are feeling and what's happening in your life, and adjust your rituals as needed.

Your whole life is a ritual. Put your heart and soul into it. Make it sacred.

Take a Moment

What appealed to you in this chapter?
What didn't appeal to you?
Did this chapter spark any ideas for you?

9

Tanja Richter

TANJA IS A massage therapist, Reiki Master, and Advanced Myoskeletal Alignment Technique Therapist who focuses on healing the body, mind, and spirit. She moved to the U.S. from Germany in 1997 and lives in Florida with her husband. She has two grown sons and a granddaughter.

"After my shower, I sit down and make a list for the day of everything I want to accomplish, ways to relax, and ways to connect with my inner child. ... I always try to do something silly and fun."

I do my ritual every day. I started it about two years ago because I felt that a morning routine would help me be more centered in myself, and I needed that.

I wake up around 5:00 or 6:00 a.m. I do some stretches for my low back while I'm still in bed, then get up and drink luke-warm water with a little lemon to help the metabolism. Then I eat cereal and drink coffee slowly and mindfully.

I exercise five days a week. Three times a week I will do about thirty minutes of cardio, and on the days in between I will do resistance training. On the weekends I take a break so that I don't burn myself out. Exercise balances my hormones and gets those endorphins flowing. It keeps me in shape both physically and mentally—it helps me stay in a happy place.

Afterward I take a shower. At the end I will do about a minute of mindful breathing techniques I learned from Thich Nhat Hanh's books. I breathe in and think, "I'm breathing in." I really feel the breath coming in and filling my belly. Then I breathe out slowly and think, "I'm breathing out." Or I might think, "I have arrived" and "I'm coming home." I do this about ten times, and I feel so much better. I also pay attention to the water hitting my head and streaming downward, and picture it washing all the negative stuff out of me and down the drain. I imagine the fresh water replenishing me with new blessings for the day. It's short but very powerful.

After my shower, I sit down and make a list for the day of everything I want to accomplish, ways to relax, and ways to con-nect with my inner child. I always do something each day to relax—maybe take a short nap—and I always try to do something silly and fun. This could include dancing around the house, hula hooping, or singing. I think it's important to keep that connection with our childish nature. When we grow up, we tend to lose it.

And then I get started with my day. I might do some extra meditation at lunch or when I come home from work; this could last from five to thirty minutes. Usually I'll listen to music. I like Liquid Mind music—it balances and calms. At the end, I might write something down that I want to work on, and then burn it to put those intentions out into the world.

Why a morning ritual is valuable to me

I started doing a morning ritual several years ago because I had a semi-breakdown. Even though I loved my family and my work, I felt torn in all directions; I was there for everyone else but me. I wasn't connected to myself, and I wasn't happy with where I was in life. I was mentally tired and physically exhausted, getting sick all the time. I began doing my ritual every day because I knew I needed it to reconnect with myself. It has made a big change in my life. I always find time every day. Even when I oversleep I try to do at least part of my routine.

We can lose who we are as we get older, marry, and have children. A morning ritual keeps your life balanced and helps protect your inner self and your connection to that self. It's a daily reassurance that you matter. Every day, it gives you time for yourself and with yourself; nobody else matters in that moment. It helps center you.

My suggestions for you

Do what you know you can incorporate each day that will not be too complicated. What will bring you joy or help you be more balanced? Start with things you have passion for or that you love to do; then you can add to that over time. My ritual didn't start out complete. I began with waking up early, drinking my coffee in peace, and doing my breathing in the shower. Then I added as I went along.

Even if it's just five minutes, like reading a page or two, it will make a difference. We can overthink things and make them too complex. Like meditation—we can make it such a big deal, like we have to sit for an hour in the lotus position to get any benefit. All we really need to do is be present. You can meditate while you're washing the dishes! I actually learned this from my husband. I used to tease him about not meditating, and he said that he did—it was just while he was mowing the grass or doing other activities. I realized that he had a good point. Those few minutes when I'm breathing in my shower make a huge difference, and it's not complicated at all.

It is so important to stay connected to ourselves throughout our entire life. Before I started my morning ritual, I put myself at the end of the list. It was always about other people. I don't want others to get to the point I did. We know early on when something is wrong. We know internally when we're overdoing it but we keep going and going, and that's when we fall apart. I hope more women will start incorporating self-care like this earlier in their lives, to keep that from happening.

Take a Moment

What appealed to you in this chapter?
What didn't appeal to you?
Did this chapter spark any ideas for you?

10
Martha Beck

MARTHA IS A best-selling author, a sociologist with three degrees from Harvard, and a life coach. As president of Martha Beck, Inc., she speaks around the world, leads teleclasses and in-person retreats, and trains other life coaches. She lives on a ranch in Central California with her family and assorted pets and wildlife.

"After breakfast I go outside on my little back deck. I sprinkle birdseed all over myself and sit very, very still in meditation. I like to be there for an hour or more; if I have time I'll sit for an hour and a half. I need at least forty minutes. Thirty minutes doesn't really even take the edge off."

I'm not a morning person, so I rely on ritual in the morning more than any other time. My doctor once said to me, "You know, you wouldn't eat the same thing for breakfast every day." And I thought, "I've eaten exactly the same thing for breakfast every day for like the last ten years!" So my morning ritual is very important and helpful to me. It goes well into the late morning; it's a long ritual, and I feel very lucky to be able to structure my day in this way.

I usually get up around 8:00 a.m., although I did have a period of sleeping later a while back. We had a somatic healer come do a retreat, and basically she told me to sleep more or die. Then everybody got very worried about me sleeping, and I slept until 9:00 every morning for months, which was good for me. But now I'm back to getting up around 8:00. It has taken me a lot of living to get to the place where I can even sleep that late, because when you've got young kids the world runs on an earlier schedule, and when you've got a job the world runs on an earlier schedule. It's really nice to have that luxury now.

When I wake up, before I even open my eyes—basically, as soon as I'm conscious—I start centering myself. I begin to be aware of my breathing and I relax so that as I think through the day I don't panic. For many years, I would wake up fully adrenalized. The entire time I was at Harvard, I would wake up gasping, like I was coming up out of water, which is not good. I don't let that happen anymore.

I lie there and I breathe, and I think, "Okay. What's going on?" If I recall a dream, I might jot highlights of it down for later analysis. Then I get up and go have a cup of tea. I used to drink coffee, but I went to Byron Katie's School for The Work, and when I came back my body would not accept coffee anymore. It was completely abrupt. I loved coffee! While I was at the school, I drank coffee every morning because it started so early, but after I got home I went for my morning cup and it just wouldn't happen. I kind of forced it down. The next day I had one sip and I gave up. I just could not swallow it. Now I have a cup of tea instead so I don't fall asleep on the meditation cushion. I'll also eat some berries and a handful of nuts; that's breakfast.

After breakfast I go outside on my little back deck. I sprinkle birdseed all over myself and sit very, very still in meditation. I like to be there for an hour or more; if I have time I'll sit for an hour and a half. I need at least forty minutes. Thirty minutes doesn't really even take the edge off. When I first started meditating, it was just twenty minutes a day, which helped some, but it didn't give me the intense experiences that I had when I finally started putting in hours at a time.

Often the chipmunks come and eat the birdseed. Sometimes they'll actually stand in my lap or even in my hands. My hands are open, palms up, and the chipmunks will just stand there and munch, and birds will come. I had three birds land on my head today, which doesn't usually happen; they usually land on my knees. So that's fun, and it's fun to be completely unsurprised and unmoving when they land on you. You have to be very relaxed because you don't see the birds coming. They just fly from the trees onto you. You have to be quite calm so as not to startle. It's good practice for regular life!

Sometimes I don't go outside to meditate because there is a narrow line between meditation and bird-watching. If I find that I'm bird-watching too much, I'll take it inside for a few days or a week.

I've never had a meditation teacher. My favorite form is Vipassana, where you focus on the breath. If anything comes to your attention—a physical sensation, thought, anything—you just name it, watch it, and let it go.

I generally meditate every day and don't skip weekends. Sometimes I won't get a chance to sit if there's something I have to do early in the day. That's not a happy thing for me, but it does happen. When I initially started meditating I was really starved for it, so for the first couple of years it was absolutely seven days a week, more than an hour every day, no exceptions. Now that I've been meditating for nearly thirty years I'm a little easier about it.

I actually first tried to meditate when I was twenty-three, but it didn't work out then. I had just finished a year at Harvard, with a small child, and I was very tired. I was going to Japan and I thought, "Might as well read something about Japan." So I got a book on Zen. At the time, meditation was not a thing that people did in the U.S. It's amazing how fast it has come on. The book gave instructions for Zen meditation, and I sat down and started trying to go through it. Within five minutes of sitting still, I had a raging fever and a rash all over my body. My throat almost closed up, and I just jumped to my feet and said out loud, "I will never do *that* again." I think I had so much repressed crap inside that when I started meditating, it all came right up. That was pretty frightening, and it was several years before I tried again.

When I travel, I like to meditate by a window so I can look out at the sky or city, but if necessary I can just sit in a room and stare at the wall as they do in Zen practice. I got to be good friends with Stephen Mitchell, whose translation of the *Tao Te Ching* is literally my favorite book. He was a Zen monk in the Korean tradition for about twenty years. Stephen informally became a Zen master for me, although we never talked about it as such.

Zen is interesting because it's so austere and unforgiving. Anything you might think about during your meditation is unimportant, for example. I learned from Stephen that the Zen approach is basically to sit and stare at the wall. With practice, you have fewer and fewer thoughts and your mind comes to rest. Vipassana is like a picnic compared to that! Stephen likes to quote Blaise Pascal, who said, "All of humanity's problems stem from man's inability to sit quietly in a room alone."

When I'm in a situation where I'm bored or frustrated—like in a doctor's waiting room or an airport—it's interesting to meditate then and get into a state of calm. Boredom is actually a trick your mind plays to hide the things it doesn't want you to see. But if you sit long enough, you get through all the boredom, and that's when the good stuff starts to happen.

Rowan Mangan, one of my favorite people, recently had a dramatic breakthrough after a long meditation. She said a lot of emotional disturbance came up, but once it cleared away there was so much less inside her mind. It feels delicious when you finally get to something they call "emptiness" in Buddhism. For Westerners, having an empty mind means you're stupid. But actually, when you get to complete emptiness, it's blissful. It's like being in the cleanest, most gorgeous space, like a beach or a meadow. It's a beautiful feeling.

After Rowan experienced this feeling, she said, "I want more *less*." That is a spiritual message in four words: I want more *less*.

When you sit long enough you get less and less, and then you want more and more less. Therefore, if you do a disciplined practice, you literally get up every day wanting less and less, more and more. It's an interesting paradox!

This feeling of less, of emptiness, is very simple—but it's not easy to access. It takes incredible rigor to get there, to be able to drop away from the stream of thoughts. And it's not that I can do it all the time, but I can peel away and take a look at it fairly consistently these days. And it's like, once you realize that space is there, it was clearly there all along. It's like you realize the sky has been touching you all the time. I mean, you're never *not* touching the sky, not ever. So that's what it's like when everything drops away—you realize that space has been holding you all along. People say stuff that's so cliché—yet when you actually experience it you realize, "Oh, there is no other way to describe this! I get what they were saying." It's very fun.

After I'm done meditating, I may write some in my journal. I recently started doing this again. I had kept a journal for years but it was super boring—like, how much I exercised. I mainly used it as a receptacle for all my anxiety. I'm actually much happier than my journals would indicate because every negative emotion would come up in the morning, and I would put it all in the journal, sort of for safekeeping.

As I got calmer over the years, there was less panic to write about. Then I got really, really happy about a year ago and didn't have anything to write. Since journaling for me is like an anxiety medication, when I'm super happy I tend not to do it at all. But I recently started again because it's nice to be able to go through my old journals and realize that nothing I was frightened of ever destroyed me. Plus, it's always interesting to see how much I exercised twelve years ago!

Next, I read some to try to get myself into a good place psychologically and, more importantly, to be able to write productively. I have a little shelf by my bed of books that comfort me, and I pick one every morning. I've had a great year, but most of my life I needed those to help calm me down.

I haven't been overwhelmed by anxiety and depression for a long, long time, but it's only because I do so many practices to get over it—which is why I always have self-help ideas! Everything I did was just trying to get past my anxiety, my depression—whatever was going on at the time—and get myself to a good place. This last year I've just been enjoying my life and my family and I haven't done as many of those self-medicating behaviors, but reading is a huge one.

I'll look at the bookshelf and think, "Hmm, which of my old friends is going to serve me today?" Then I'll pick the book that feels right and I'll poke through it and turn to different pages. They're all heavily underlined and annotated. I'll go to a page that grabs my attention and keep reading until I find something that makes me feel happy.

Most of them are spiritual books. A couple might be called creativity books, but mainly they're clustered around the topics of awakening and enlightenment. So I get myself a good dose of that.

Next, I make a day plan with my loved ones. We sit around together and everybody says what they have to do. Since we live on a ranch in the middle of nowhere, we have to figure out stuff like who's going to drive into town that day and what we need. So there's the necessary pragmatic aspect of it, and then we also try to make sure everybody has something in the day that makes them happy. It's lovely. It's a bonding experience, like many families bond over dinner. For us, bonding over planning the day is incredible. Then I get to work and that's the end of the morning.

Why a ritual is valuable to me

All of my morning ritual is preparation for writing, because the hardest work I do is writing. I do a lot of different things, but by far the hardest is writing. All of this is just to get me to the point where I'll sit down and write something. Without it I can't keep going; it's all a way of nerving myself up to get to the page.

The meditation part is extraordinarily transformative. I bet almost every culture has a tradition of meditation in it somewhere because somebody stumbled over the fact that if you just sit still and breathe, things get better. It's a very slow process, but it positively affects your whole life. For example, I used to wake up terrified and gasping, and now if a bird lands on my head I just sit there. I don't even wince.

It creates a real shift. You enter a different state of being. Meditating puts my whole body in a parasympathetic nervous state instead of a sympathetic one, which means that my whole body is less tense, less stressed, less sick, less likely to be in chronic pain. There's no question that it has immense benefits.

I'm healthier in all kinds of ways, but the biggest thing is just being able to access a state of calm. That is not what most people put on their vision boards. Mostly we say we want happiness and bliss and joy. However, calm is incredible; just feeling calm makes such a difference. The thing about meditation is, especially when you do it for longer periods, it makes your whole life calmer.

For example, if you put a group of meditators and non-meditators in a room and measure their autonomic responses after the sound of a gunshot, those who haven't been meditating will freak out and not remember much about the incident, whereas the people who have been meditating will just sit there and notice everything that happens. So their observational powers are opened up and their startle response is greatly reduced. If you paint that brush over your whole life, it's amazing how different things are.

My suggestions for you

I know it sounds so boring, but if I had just one thing that I could scream from the rooftops, it would be, "Please, please, please let yourself get enough sleep. It will wreck your life if you don't." I recommend to everyone to make sure by whatever means necessary that you're getting enough sleep. You can start with getting to bed earlier. A morning ritual will not benefit your life if you're not sleeping enough.

There's this overwhelming intensity in our culture where we say, "I'll just get up an hour earlier, that can't hurt." But it can hurt. I had so many health problems for so long because I wasn't sleeping enough. If you need to use an alarm, regularly hit the snooze button, and rush into your day, you probably aren't getting to bed early enough to wake up naturally. So put your health first. Don't give up sleep for anything.

Be considerate of your own biorhythms. Some people are morning people and some are not. Maybe the reason people are so dramatically different, with nighttime people and daytime people, is that back when we were living in nature, exposed to predators, we needed someone watching the fire all the time who needed to be not just awake but alert. I still see this when I go to Africa, where there are very dangerous predators all around. So it makes good sense that some people are alert in the morning and some people are alert at night. There's only a certain amount you can play with nature. Don't fight biology if you don't have to.

Next, start with very, very, very small bits of noticing how you feel in the morning and what you would like to do. Your ritual has to be your own and not somebody else's. I started meditating for an hour and a half every morning because I desperately wanted to, not because anybody told me to. I'm not a big one for forcing anything.

Try to cultivate a feeling of calm presence. As you're drinking your coffee, as you're getting in your car, or as you're walking to go somewhere, breathe deeply and see what would be nicer. Observe how you are in the morning and then take tender loving care of that person. See what that person wants.

Observe yourself, trust yourself, and give yourself what you want. Like Goethe said, "As soon as you trust yourself, you will know how to live." That's it. That will lead you to finding the right ritual and the life that satisfies you.

TAKE A MOMENT

What appealed to you in this chapter?
What didn't appeal to you?
Did this chapter spark any ideas for you?

11

Stacy Wooster

STACY IS A massage and yoga therapist, astrologer, and herbalist who helps others embrace a holistic life. She lives in Austin, Texas, with her husband and three children.

"The morning sets the tone for the whole day. ... If we can begin in a more conscious way, we are able to make choices that are more aware. It's a totally different feel. And all the small choices add up; it's the subtle things that really change our lives."

In the morning we all do a routine—we get up, brush our teeth, put on clothes. Yet if we don't do it mindfully, our routine runs us instead of us running our routine.

My morning routine focuses on getting in touch with my body. I lie in bed for a minute after awakening, breathe, and notice how I'm feeling in each area—where there might be tightness, for instance. I take the time to see what comes up.

Next, I do yoga. I like to do it first thing in the morning so I can start the day centered and grounded. I have a dedicated space where I keep my mat and props so I can go right to it.

My practice is usually pretty quick. I used to think I needed a seventy-five-minute session, but the reality of my life is that I don't have time for that, especially in the morning. I have three children, and one needs to be dropped off for school carpool by 7:00 a.m., so mornings are go time. Instead of one longer session, I break it up into five-to-fifteen minute chunks throughout the day.

I start by lying on my back and just feeling the ground. I do some simple movements while lying there, like stretching my legs and twisting. I then revisit it throughout the day—I might fit in a more active practice around midday, when my body is looser.

I do some self-massage when I can, always making sure that my motions pull back toward the heart to help with venous circulation. Sometimes the massage might be really quick, like just a few minutes of rubbing in some lotion. I use a lotion with lavender; it smells good and acts as a sensory cue to relax. Scent works with the limbic system, a primal part of our brain, and can evoke powerful memories or associations. When we do something repeatedly, like caring for ourselves with massage, and incorporate a certain scent, it trains our brain to associate the two. Each time we smell that scent, subconsciously we begin to relax.

I like to add a magnesium salt spray to my lotion so that the magnesium can be absorbed through my skin. Magnesium is something that many of us are deficient in, and this is a more gentle way of getting it than taking supplements, which can be hard on the digestive system.

I make sure that the lotions I use have the simplest ingredients and the least amount of chemicals possible, since whatever we put on our skin is absorbed and processed by the body. If I can't pronounce the word, I don't want it on my skin and in my body!

I might also dry brush my skin before my shower, and those motions always go toward the heart as well. Dry brushing boosts lymphatic flow and circulation, and helps the body flush out toxins. It also gently exfoliates and brightens the skin.

Why a morning ritual is valuable to me

A body awareness or meditation practice in the morning gives me a baseline to measure against throughout the day. I might notice I have tension in my shoulders that wasn't there earlier, or realize that it was easy to breathe deeply in the morning, but now it's harder. I'm able to see how I've changed, and then respond to that.

Throughout the day I will do quick body scans and notice how I'm feeling. Since I've been cultivating awareness of my body for a long time, I know how it feels when I'm tense in a certain area. Then I try to link the sensation—I think back to what I did or what happened earlier in the day that might have caused that tension. I can then take steps to counteract it. For instance, if I notice that I'm feeling tight and anxious, I might do kaki pranayama breath to calm down. In English it's called "beak breath," and it is a soothing technique. (To do it, inhale through your nose, then purse your lips into an O as if you were drinking from a straw and exhale. The elongated exhalation helps bring about the relaxation response. Repeat until you feel calmer.)

The morning sets the tone for the whole day. If we get up and are "go, go, go" right away, that's the pace for the rest of the day. If we can begin in a more conscious way, we are able to make choices that are more aware. It's a totally different feel. And all the small choices add up; it's the subtle things that really change our lives.

Rituals also give us something to lean on when times get tough. A teacher I follow, Manorama, says, "We don't need our practice every day, but when we need it, we hope we've been practicing every day." Rituals help us through upsetting times or transitions, like moving or having a baby—experiences that are good but can still register as traumatic because they're life changing. Everyone has those, and everyone faces challenging situations. If we have rituals already in place, we're more prepared and better able to cope.

My suggestions for you

Make your ritual accessible so you can do it consistently. If you're going to do a movement practice, put your mat and props right by the bed or in the space you're going to use them so you can get to them easily.

Keep it simple. Something easy to start with is just to take ten slow breaths while you're still in bed. Then when you sit up, put your feet on the floor and feel them there. The feet have a lot of nerve endings; paying attention to how they feel on the floor helps you be more aware of your body and grounds you.

Start with something that fits your schedule and that you know you can repeat. We tend to try to do too much at once. Then we can't keep it up, and we feel guilty. You could try a tiered approach—take the ten breaths and feel your feet for a week or so, then add a practice.

They say it takes twenty-one days to form a habit, but it really takes closer to sixty. It's very hard for us to incorporate something new. We tend to fall back into our old patterns. Tracking yourself can help—write down what you do each day in your calendar.

Don't stress yourself out trying to make time for a long practice. You can make little moments of awareness and self-care throughout your day. You can do a quick body scan, and if you feel any issues, backtrack a little to see what the cause might be. Then do something like self-massage or a breathing technique to address it so it doesn't get worse. Awareness gives you choice. It allows you to change things; otherwise, you're just going through the motions.

You don't have to have a perfect dedicated space; that's not always practical. Find a spot that's accessible and easy. If you're going to try a sitting practice like meditating, I recommend having a chair available. It can be hard to sit on the floor in the morning when your body is stiff from sleeping. Using a chair can make it easier to meditate because you're not asking as much from the body.

And whatever you do, congratulate yourself when you're done! Celebrate it. Tell yourself, "Hey, I did ten slow breaths—awesome! Great job!" Encouragement will help you keep going.

Take a Moment

What appealed to you in this chapter?
What didn't appeal to you?
Did this chapter spark any ideas for you?

12

Patricia Charpentier

PATRICIA IS A multi–award-winning author. Through her business Writing Your Life, she has helped hundreds of people create a written legacy for their families and generations to come. She works as a coach, ghostwriter, editor, and publisher, and travels the country presenting workshops and presentations on memoir writing. She lives in Orlando, Florida, with her husband.

"Think about what you enjoy and do that. Don't do something just because others recommend it. Do what makes you happy."

One of the greatest joys of being my own boss is not having to use an alarm clock—that starts my day off right! I wake up naturally between 6:45 and 7:15 a.m. I can't get up any earlier; it just doesn't work for me.

My husband is a morning person. He rises at 5:00 a.m. every day. He's got his own routine. Often he's out golfing by the time I get up. But if he's in the house, I might say, "I'm doing my practice for the next hour and a half," and he's respectful of that.

I've had morning practices at various times throughout my life, but lately I've gotten much more consistent. I have started the day with a prayer for the last twenty-five years or so. It's a conscious process of giving the day over to a higher power. I ask to be led to say and do whatever will best serve those I encounter, and to bring kindness to the people whose paths I cross. For about the last fifteen years, I have also read from a little book with meditations and thoughts for the day.

I've expanded my morning ritual over the past several years. With the guidance of my mentor, Lezlie Laws (chapter 17), I've gotten it more defined. I still start with a prayer focused on turning the day over, but I've also added a few practices.

First, while I eat my breakfast I read intentions I have written. There are about ten to twenty of them, focused on various areas of my life. They change over time. Some get added, some get taken away.

Then I read three prayers; they're about turning over my day, letting go of financial insecurity, and asking for relief from any defects of character.

Next, I write. I use a website, 750words.com, which is a digital variation of the morning pages from *The Artist's Way* by Julia Cameron. It's a great tool to keep me writing—it sends reminders, and you get badges when you write a certain number of days in a row. I really respond to that kind of motivation. I'll turn myself inside out to get that little digital badge!

My writing is focused on gratitude first. Next, I set intentions about how I want to live that day and how I can give my best to my clients and projects. Then I will ask the universe for the answer to a question or problem I have. The answer doesn't always come right away, but I find that the act of asking orients me toward finding the solution. It's very helpful.

I will also do a thought or emotion dump, where I put everything I'm currently thinking or feeling down on the page so I can get rid of it. I might do this first, so I can get that out of the way, or I might do it last. It just depends on how I'm feeling that day. I also might use part of this time to write my memoir or something for work.

Recently, I added something else to my ritual. I was having trouble finding the time to learn about new things, whether it was for work or just something I was curious about. So now I'll also read a blog post or listen to a podcast—something short.

My morning ritual is a sacred time for me. If there's something I really want to do, I have a better chance if I add it to this time. I find it's much more effective to attach new things to an existing habit rather than create new habits.

Last, I'll do a guided meditation. I use a website called Calm.com, which posts a new ten-to-fifteen-minute meditation every day. It's great. I've always struggled with meditating, but this makes me look forward to it every day.

When I travel, I might not be able to manage my full ritual, but I try to do at least some parts of it. I used to be very rigid about getting my writing done every day. I think I was up to five hundred days in a row at one point! But now I might miss it occasionally, and it's okay, although I don't like when it happens.

I also have a nighttime practice. I will write in my five-year journal, which gives six lines per day and is laid out so you can see what you wrote on that day in previous years. Next, I'll say some prayers of gratitude, and then my husband and I will tell each other something that occurred that day that we feel grateful for, which often sparks a conversation.

Why a morning ritual is important to me

My ritual starts my day off right. It puts me in a place where I'm a lot more focused and calm. If I get sucked into checking email first, I'm gone. Then I'm in multitasking mode and I'm hopping from thing to thing. A set practice helps me focus on one item at a time, which sets the tone for the day. I'm more mindful of my choices and where I'm putting my time and energy.

My suggestions for you

Start with something doable. Be realistic about how much time you really have. Doing something for five minutes each day consistently is better than doing an hour every four days.

Also, know yourself. I'd love to be able to get up an hour earlier and fit more in, but I know that I don't want it badly enough to make it stick. Know your priorities and work within that.

Think about what you enjoy and do that. Don't do something just because others recommend it. Do what makes you happy. Maybe it's something as simple and fun as coloring. Maybe it's something else. What will make a difference in your life?

Pick something you can feel successful about right away. Commit to it for a short period of time—make it easy on yourself, like, "I'll read for ten minutes for the next three mornings." Then look at your schedule to see what might interfere, and figure out how to work around any issues. It's easy to get discouraged if you don't do what you say you're going to, so set yourself up for success. Once you've been doing it a while and it's a habit, you can add on if you want.

TAKE A MOMENT

What appealed to you in this chapter?
What didn't appeal to you?
Did this chapter spark any ideas for you?

13

Char Cooper

CHAR IS A businesswoman who recently sold the industrial distribution company that she founded more than twenty years ago. She continues to consult for that company. Also, as an avid runner, she enjoys competing in marathons and half-marathons. Char lives in Indiana with her husband and has three children and three grandchildren.

"Having a morning ritual, I believe, is the key to stepping up to the starting line of a new adventure. Every day is full of possibility. You don't know what it will bring. ... [Mine] gives me the ability to meet the day's activities in the best possible way for myself and for my family."

I get up around 6:00 a.m. or earlier—rarely after—and put on my running clothes. Running is a key element in my morning ritual. When I run, those days are the best. If I sleep in or don't have time to run, I feel a little uneasy all day. I feel a little frustrated that I haven't given that gift to myself.

Now that my kids are grown and I'm semi-retired, I have more flexibility in my days without as many outside obligations. This allows me the opportunity to pursue my passions: running, spending time with family and friends, and learning and growing through a variety of experiences. I've been running for twenty-two years and doing it in a focused and competitive manner for the past seven or eight years.

To kick off the morning before my run, I eat a healthy and nutritious breakfast. I love breakfast; it's my favorite meal of the day. I usually have Kashi GoLean cereal topped with strawberries, bananas, and blueberries. Sometimes I'll also have a scrambled egg. Then I have a cappuccino—just one! It's my only caffeine of the day and is sure to get me fired up for the excitement of the day ahead!

I will check my email to see if anything needs to be addressed immediately and then attend to any pressing responsibilities—at least those that need to be taken care of at 6:00 a.m.! After that, I take off on my run. I have a training plan, so I run according to that—sometimes intense, sometimes more relaxed—and always with a goal for the miles to be covered that day.

It's a bonus to be outside right before dawn. I love the peace, calmness, and quiet when almost everyone else is asleep and there's virtually no traffic. It's beautiful to be running just as the sun comes up. The sunrise is so inspiring to me.

While I'm on the path, my thoughts always turn to grati-tude—not only that I'm healthy and able to be running strong, but also that I have such fantastic things in my life, including amazing and loving family and friends. It's a magical morn-ing period of reflection, thankfulness, and looking forward to what's ahead.

My running time gives a fresh start to each day. Running focuses my mind, gets my blood pumping, and gets my brain cells moving. I come up with some of my best ideas during my morning runs. It also helps me remember things I need to do that I might otherwise have forgotten!

I run six days a week. On Saturday mornings my husband and I hang out and make a special breakfast together, so no running—just hubby time! When I'm traveling for business or pleasure, I always try to fit my miles in, even if I have to get up earlier or run in an area that's a little iffy.

I run rain or shine, in scorching hot or freezing cold weather—down to zero degrees as long as it's not icy! I love being out in nature. If I wake up and I'm not feeling so great—a bit sluggish or headachey—I run anyway because I know it will make me feel better. And it always does!

Why a morning ritual is valuable to me

Having a morning ritual, I believe, is the key to stepping up to the starting line of a new adventure. Every day is full of possi-bility. You don't know what it will bring. With shoes laced tight and a healthy breakfast and cappuccino downed, stepping out to the running paths sets me up to be able to handle whatever happens in that day, whether it's a celebration or a challenge. It gives me the ability to meet the day's activities in the best possible way for myself and for my family.

My suggestions for you

Think about what you truly enjoy doing. If you were given a half hour in which you could do whatever you wanted, what would you choose? Perhaps that activity is how you want to start your day. One of my friends gets up early to read because that's what she loves. Another likes to just sit and drink her coffee alone. Think about what makes you happiest and then try to incorporate it into your morning. That daily gift to yourself will make the twenty-four hours ahead especially sweet!

Take a Moment

What appealed to you in this chapter?
What didn't appeal to you?
Did this chapter spark any ideas for you?

14

Wendy Battino

WENDY IS A life coach, endorsed intuitive energy reader, and health and wellness coach who uses a variety of tools, including nature, to help people map out their right path. She lives in Alaska with her husband, three dogs, and a cat in a log cabin they built by hand.

"Getting outside is a powerful way to get grounded instantly. No matter where you live, you can find nature—even in the busiest and biggest cities like London, you can find something natural to connect with."

I don't wake up at the same time every day; I love to change it up. I probably wake up at 5:00 a.m. about once a week, 6:00 or 7:00 often, and then I sleep in until 9:00 about once a week. Sleeping in might not always happen on a weekend—sometimes it's a weekday! That's part of my intention for how I want to live. I loathed having to be on a schedule when I was a teacher. I like to feel free to go with my own clock; it's so powerful to make your own schedule. My husband makes his own schedule too. Each day is different, depending on what's going on, and we really enjoy that.

I tend to get nervous if my life is too safe and repetitive, but I will do a ritual almost every morning. While the specifics may vary, I make a point of going outside and touching the ground every day. It's powerful to do something physical to connect to the earth in the morning. I step outside barefoot, regardless of the weather. Even if it's forty degrees below zero, I can at least stand on the porch for a little bit, or I can scoop up some snow and wash my face with it.

Most mornings, I go out to a shaman circle that I built on the pathway to our house. It's about three to four feet around, made of rocks that I embedded into the ground. I collected slate stones from a special spot and put them on the outside of the circle, with white stones on the inside. It's my grounding and centering place. I will stand in the circle and turn to face each of the four directions. It varies as to exactly what I do—whatever calls to me that day—but generally I face north and acknowledge it, and then do each direction in turn. I have a variety of practices related to this—a sort of toolbox I've created over the years. Sometimes I only have a few minutes, so I quickly face each direction and say hello. Other days, I spend a long time in each direction.

I believe the universe is communicating to us always and showing us our own wisdom. This practice is a way for me to connect to that. Sometimes I'll ask an open question, like,

"North, what guidance do you have for me today?" Or I might ask a question about a particular issue I'm working on.

The other day I was having trouble picking the right image for the cover of my book, so I asked about that. The book is about my Alaskan husky, Luzy. She was inside the house at the time, but she knows how to open the door. She did that and ran across my field of vision with her tongue hanging out, all happy and carefree—so I got the message that the cover should show her at play!

I will set an intention while I'm in the circle, and feel into which direction will help me the most with that intention. Then, after my ritual, before I start work, I try to do one action that ties into my intention. For example, if my intention is to get healthier, I will do one tiny thing to support that. Often we set intentions but don't put any energy into actually realizing them; I like to take a step toward it right away.

When I'm done in the circle, I go inside and sit on my pillow to meditate. I used to try to meditate first, but that didn't work as well. It's much better if I go outside first. Meditation lets my mind practice resting. I sit for long periods—an hour when I can. When I'm antsy, I'll get up and take a walking meditation. The goal is to let my thoughts go. Sometimes I succeed! It's hard to not think, but I try to let the thoughts happen and then go away. Often my dogs and cat are draped all around me as I meditate. They don't disturb me, they just relax. Our energy affects those around us—sometimes I'll lead a group meditation of ten people and the dogs will just chill.

After meditating, if I don't have clients or calls first thing, I'll take the dogs out for a hike, run, or swim (in the summer). I like to move my body in a fun way.

At some point in the morning, I drink coffee. It's always on—I love the smell! I usually drink it after meditation, but there are some mornings I need it right away!

When I travel, I have a compass on my iPhone that I use to determine the directions where I am so I can do the greeting ritual. If I'm in a hotel room, I'll just turn in a circle. If I'm out camping, I will look for a beautiful spot.

Sometimes travel or emergencies can prevent me from doing a full ritual in the morning, but before I go to bed that night I at least have to check in with north and west—those are my favorite directions.

I first started being aware of the directions when I worked as an archaeologist in California in my early twenties, before I moved to Alaska. I would be in the middle of nowhere looking for sites, using a compass and a map (this was before GPS). Interestingly, every site I found had an orientation to it—it was built along either a north-south or east-west line. I would play with this. When I was camping I would pay attention to how it felt to sleep with my head pointing different directions. When I woke up, I would notice which direction I was facing. I got very into meditation and would go on silent retreats for up to two weeks at a time, and I would face and feel the different directions when sitting in meditation.

Later in my twenties, I came to Alaska as an archaeologist. I later became a teacher, but I learned way more than I taught. At one point, I was living in a Native Alaskan village, and I would go off and explore the woods all the time. Many times when I was out there, I would run into a particular Native man, and he would just walk away. But finally he started walking with me and talking to me. He taught me how he thought of the directions as having particular energies: north is wisdom;

east is kindness; south lights up the dark; and west is forward movement, next steps, and the spiritual realm. When he would hunt, he would ask for favors from the different directions.

For a long time, my practice of greeting the directions was something I did privately. I just started sharing it with clients over the past few years. It's interesting—as I've started offering this practice to others, they make it their own.

I think it's important that we keep growing our rituals as we grow, to change them to accommodate our changes. Recently I've been experiencing some symptoms, like an occasional foggy brain, that may be the beginnings of perimenopause. I'm fascinated by this phase and am collecting stories and practices from all over the world about it, looking for the power. I want to make it a good experience. So lately in my grounding practice, I'm being specific about checking in with the various parts of myself and how I'm feeling. When I face north, which has to do with the mind, I might ask, "Do I feel foggy today?" Facing east, which relates to the emotions, I might ask, "How am I emotionally?" When I face south, which is the body, "What am I feeling physically?" And when facing west, which is spirit, "What's going on with my spiritual energy?"

It's powerful to acknowledge exactly where we are and to accept how we're feeling—and to ask, "What's the gift in this?" It's another level of the same ritual—taking a deeper step into touching base with myself. It's fun to start with something simple and then allow your soul to deepen and alter it so it stays relevant to you and your current situation. It's very powerful to see how it evolves.

Why a morning ritual is valuable to me

I love morning rituals because they help me envision what I want to create. They get me deeply in touch with my center and help me ground myself so I can see more clearly. If I then keep my eye on that vision and stay grounded, I believe I can create anything I want with that focus.

When I don't do my morning ritual, I feel off center. Things are confusing. Communication doesn't go well and I can't find my flow.

When I'm not grounded, I get more and more worried about what others are doing. I can also get into the mode of trying to manipulate and control things around me.

When I'm grounded and I read something horrible in the news, I feel sadness, but I can also think of ways to help others and myself. When I'm not grounded, I feel it all too deeply. I can get overwhelmed by upsetting news.

Being grounded also helps me be more intuitive. I can communicate with nature. I can hear the animals and be aware of what's going on with them. If I'm out in the wilderness and run into a bear, I have to be completely aware, or it's dangerous.

It's much more empowering to be grounded. I have better relationships. I realize everything isn't about me—when people are upset, it's not about me. Also, if others are praising me, that's not all about me either. I don't lose my head. It helps me not get off track.

I also see clear benefits to my coaching business—when I'm grounded and authentic, I have more clients. If I'm spinning, I don't attract as many.

I'm better able to set and achieve my goals—it's hard to get clear on intentions when we're not grounded. It's hard for my goals to come to me. For example, I really wanted to build my own log cabin. I was very definite about it. Then I met my husband, and he wanted to as well! We could picture it and we had a clear vision. That helped us achieve our goal, even though we didn't have any building experience. Because we had no doubts in our minds, we were able to ignore the naysayers and build our cabin, which we live in today.

The wonderful thing about this life is that we can create the life we want, whatever it is. I was born in San Francisco, so I was a city girl, but I had always wanted to live in the wilderness. I now live in a town of about seven hundred people north of Anchorage. We also have a homestead that is accessible only by plane. Then about fifteen years ago, my husband and I decided we both wanted to travel and enjoy some city time as well. We created an educational nonprofit foundation that had us traveling all over the world. We created that with a clear vision and intention, and it wouldn't have been possible if we hadn't stayed grounded.

My suggestions for you

Set your intention and focus your energy on it. Create the life you want; otherwise, you get swayed by others' energies. Grounding gives you the space to see what it is you want, and getting outside is a powerful way to get grounded instantly. No matter where you live, you can find nature—even in the busiest and biggest cities like London, you can find something natural to connect with.

Women are told what we can and can't do. Having a morning ritual gets you space to listen to yourself and find out what you want. Ask yourself, "Who am I?" "What sparks me?" "What comes across my field of vision that's appealing to me?" The world is loud. Social media, television, newspapers, magazines—it can be dangerous if you're not centered. You can get buffeted about by everyone else's opinions and desires.

Setting intentions is so powerful; I believe that just thinking of what we want physically creates it on another plane. Then we have to catch up on our plane and bring it into our current reality. That's why it's crucial to ground ourselves and master our thoughts about things. We have this ability to create, but it takes intention. Our practices can help us find that focus. Everything I've focused on and achieved feels like a miracle. The ability to create the life we love—exactly what we want—is so amazing.

Lately I've been visioning about how to bring people up here for adventures but not have to plan it all—I'm not a detail person, and when I led a retreat up here last year I got sick afterward because I worked too hard on it. So my dream is to lead a retreat without having to deal with the details. A friend just called about hiring me to coach at a retreat that she is holding—and she will handle all the planning! Now I'm thinking, "What else do I want?"

Why do I keep getting surprised when my desires happen? What I'm learning is that we need to keep thinking bigger and bigger *and* have a practice where we can focus on what we want.

I know that what I like to do might not appeal to everyone, but I hope it inspires you to think of your own wacky ideas. What kind of life do you want to create? Make time to dream about it, create a clear vision, stay grounded as you pursue it, and you can achieve it.

Take a Moment

What appealed to you in this chapter?
What didn't appeal to you?
Did this chapter spark any ideas for you?

15

Holly Shoebridge

Holly took the gorgeous photo on this book's cover. Believe it or not, photography is just a hobby for her. She is also an accountant and recently launched a company serving creative businesses. She lives in Sydney, Australia, with her husband and Australian bulldog.

"I love meditating because it helps me center myself. It teaches me to observe my emotions rather than act impulsively. It helps me slow down and process situations rather than fly off the handle. … I use it to get on top of my anxiety—it's essential—and doing it every day has created such a huge shift."

I started photographing ocean sunrises in about 2010. At the time, I was living across from the beach and waking up very early. I was experiencing some epic anxiety and would go there after I woke up to help calm me down. Then I decided that because I was up early and already there, I might as well start taking pictures. I got a camera and just started playing around with it—I thought photography would be a cool hobby. It made me really happy, so I created a website, Facebook page, and Instagram account to share that happiness with others.

The forty-five minutes before the sun rises is the best time of day to me—it's quite peaceful. I love being out on the beach then. When you're alone like that, it gives you time for introspection, and I started learning a lot about myself. I began writing little inspirational messages to go along with the photographs when I posted them.

Now I live about a five minutes' drive from the beach, so I don't go out there every morning to photograph. I meditate and walk my dog instead. Meditation and movement are essential for a great start to my day. I usually wake up between 4:00 and 5:30 a.m. I've always been a morning person, but I've been getting up this early for about the last eight or nine years.

I begin by drinking two big glasses of water with lemon, and while I'm doing that the kettle is boiling for coffee. I love coffee! I'll drink some, then sit for meditation.

I love meditating because it helps me center myself. It teaches me to observe my emotions rather than act impulsively. It helps me slow down and process situations rather than fly off the handle.

Meditation allows us to feel what's going on around us— the world is such a peaceful place. I think we create a lot of unnecessary excitement and pain, and meditation helps us get back to connecting with that peace.

I've meditated off and on for about ten years, but since the start of 2017 it has been every day. I use it to get on top of my anxiety—it's essential—and doing it every day has created such a huge shift. I meditate for about ten to twenty minutes on the weekdays, and more like thirty minutes on the weekends. If I have longer I will take longer, but I'm more likely to do two shorter sessions than to sit for one long one.

First, I sit down and feel my body against the floor. As I sit there I calm down, focus, and follow my breathing. Thoughts pop up and I just observe them and let them go. After a while they start to simmer down. Then I'm left with that sense of vast openness, which is really what we meditate for.

While I'm meditating, my dog will sit by me or lay his head on my lap. When I'm done, I'll take him out and we'll go for a run around the park and throw the ball. It's a very fun start to the day. I think it's so important to move and get exercise.

Then I come home and have an epic breakfast—I like berries, Mueslix, coconut, and almond milk. I tend to eat after I meditate. I'd read that a lot of Buddhist monks meditate on an empty stomach to keep them more alert, so I follow that. After breakfast I'll go to work, either at the office or at home.

Why a morning ritual is valuable to me

I think a morning ritual is valuable because the way we start the day is the way the rest of our day will continue. Beginning with self-care and a good breakfast and exercise is so essential to our health and happiness. If you do that every day, every day is going to be awesome.

My suggestions for you

Everyone is different; not everyone wants to get up before dawn like me! But if you're a morning person, try to get up a little earlier to make some time for yourself. If you're not, do whatever works for your schedule. Allow time to relax and do something that's just for you.

What do you love? Maybe it's walking your dog or spending time in your garden. Whatever it is, find thirty or forty-five minutes to do it. Even fifteen minutes will make a big difference. Center yourself in something you love.

And then make sure you eat a good breakfast! If you get busy later in the day and can't eat well, at least you will have had something nutritious at the start!

TAKE A MOMENT

What appealed to you in this chapter?
What didn't appeal to you?
Did this chapter spark any ideas for you?

16
Jeanne Geier Lewis

JEANNE IS A start-up entrepreneur and co-founder of Creativebug, a website with more than a thousand video art lessons, and Capsure, an app for sharing personal moments privately. She lives in the San Francisco Bay area with her husband and two children.

"I recently went three days without meditating and I was miserable. I started doubting myself, felt anxious, and got stressed about stuff that doesn't usually bother me. It affected every part of my life. It was an affirmation of how much meditation is helping me—sometimes it's hard to see what a difference something is making until you stop."

If I wake up and look at the phone right away, my whole day is wrecked. I have to meditate first. Meditation needs to happen before anything else; that's my time.

I wake up before the rest of my family. Since my husband is asleep next to me, rather than moving around and possibly waking him and everyone else, I just stay in bed. I'll sit up and begin meditating.

I practice Transcendental Meditation, in which you focus on repeating a mantra. The mantra is a tool to distract you. Your mind is like a young child and the mantra is a toy you give it to keep it occupied so you can get to the deep work. The mantra also works as a cue to let your body know it's time to relax.

As I start, I imagine there's a Ferris Wheel in my mind, and each car has a thought. I'm the ride operator and as each car comes by, I help the thought off and say, "Thanks for visiting. See you later!" Finally, all the seats are empty, and then I transcend. It's similar to how you feel when you're about to fall asleep—you're not fully conscious. To me, it's like diving deep into the ocean and floating back up slowly.

I meditate for twenty minutes. I use the clock app on my phone and put it in front of me so I can peek and check the time, but generally I don't need it. I will naturally open my eyes after about twenty minutes. I don't like to use any sort of sound to signal the end—it's too jarring.

In Transcendental Meditation, you "come out" three to five minutes before you get up from your session. This stage is really important. You've been in an in-between state, and you can give yourself a headache if you come out of it too abruptly. It's like someone jolting you awake; you're foggy and disoriented. During this transitional time, you don't keep repeating your mantra. I usually say the rosary. It's second nature to me, so it's an easy way to come back into awareness. Sometimes, however, I will lie down and go back to sleep!

If I have a problem I want to work through, I'll ask for help with it before I start. I meditate knowing that I will be guided in a way that makes sense. Then the problems tend to work out without my having to try so hard.

I've started using an app called Sattva to track my sessions. I love keeping score with myself. When I open it and it says, "You have a seventy-three-day streak," that makes me feel good and I want to keep the streak going.

After I'm done meditating, it's still my quiet time. I get up and make coffee or tea, and give all my attention to that as I drink it. Then I jump into the day.

When I was with my first start-up, Creativebug, I didn't have this set morning practice and I was not taking care of myself. I sacrificed my health and time with my family. After I sold Creativebug, I decided I wouldn't do any more start-ups because of that. Then this opportunity to create Capsure came, and I really believed in it. So this time I've committed to taking care of myself. I meditate two times a day no matter what—first thing in the morning and again at midday for a boost. I'm also eating healthy and not putting work before my life. It's so much better this time, and it's all because of meditation.

I believe that our energy affects others around us, and when you meditate, you create a positive atmosphere around yourself. I went to a Transcendental Meditation retreat last year and there was a woman in the class who worked at a big tech firm. She said that when she started practicing TM, she noticed a ripple effect across her team even though she hadn't discussed it with anyone. Events in her department started going more smoothly, things were getting done more easily, and there was no drama. The changes in her were affecting everyone on her team.

When I was younger, I worked at Time, Inc. I hated public speaking and would get really stressed whenever I had to do it. Next, I started Creativebug and had to be out there promoting. Then I sold it and had to negotiate with CEOs and lawyers. That was all really hard for me. At the time, I had an app for a centering meditation, and I would do it before important phone calls or discussions. It was how I coped; it allowed me to remove myself from the intensity of the situation. I would set an intention for how I wanted the conversation to go and would act it out in my head in advance. I would ask, "Please let my higher self speak to their higher self." One time I did this right before I got on the phone with a very important guy who did not want to do what I wanted. During the call, he said almost verbatim what I had envisioned in the meditation. I thought, "Wow, this is real!"

When I was trying to fund Capsure, every investor I knew had said no, and I was down to the last one. My co-founder and I were headed to the meeting and I told him, "This is the last person I have to reach out to. I'm leaving it up to the universe." When we first got there, the investor told us that the idea didn't fit his investing philosophy, so he just wanted to talk. But I started pitching anyway, making it personal to him. My presentation included the amount that I felt was the right number for him; my co-founder had said earlier that we should ask for more, to which I replied, "No, this is his number." It was instinct. As I was talking to the investor, he asked to see the funding slide. When he saw it, he said, "Is that the number?" and I told him yes. He said, "Okay, I can do that." So now I feel like I'm just going to get out of my own way!

Why a morning ritual is valuable to me

Meditation makes me more aware. I'm better at holding my tongue when I'm mad; I don't speak out of anger. I'm hyper aware of being critical, and I'm better at empathizing with others. I can tend to make snap judgments about people and I don't like that. TM helps me to be nonjudgmental.

It also helps me be less controlling. Instead of trying to manage every aspect of life, I will set an intention and roll with it. I still have to be active, look for signs, and work on my goals, but it's a more relaxed approach.

If I didn't meditate, I'd feel frazzled all day. It's like, "Wait, what am I doing?" It's hard to know what to prioritize. The morning meditation puts me in a focused mindset; then the midday meditation gives me a boost and makes the rest of the day go more smoothly.

I recently went three days without meditating and I was miserable. I started doubting myself, felt anxious, and got stressed about stuff that doesn't usually bother me. It affected every part of my life. It was an affirmation of how much meditation is helping me—sometimes it's hard to see what a difference something is making until you stop.

My suggestions for you

There are different religions and different practices, and they're all worthwhile—they're just various paths to the same place. It's like flavors of ice cream. Do you prefer pistachio ice cream or mango sorbet? What do you like best? You choose whatever works for you.

Of course, I highly recommend Transcendental Meditation, as it has been so effective for me. I find it easier than the Zen approach. Also, you don't have to sit in a particular position, so you can do it anywhere—even in a mall or an airport. All you have to do is close your eyes and focus on your mantra. Some people use headphones to help block out noise if they're in a public place, but as you continue to practice, you won't even need that. The sounds just fade away.

Whatever ritual you choose, try to find some time to sit in silence each day. I went to a retreat where I meditated in silence six hours a day for six days. It made me realize how incredibly noisy the world is. When I was driving home, I was on sensory overload; everything just seemed so loud. We have become numb to it, but it's good to spend a few minutes each day without all of that stimulation.

When you're taking time for yourself, try not to be disturbed or distracted, like by notifications on your phone. At that meditation retreat, I learned that it can take twenty minutes for your body to recover when you're interrupted while concentrating. And even after that time, you can't really get back into the state of flow you were in. When I'm meditating, and also when I'm working on something that requires concentration, I'll shut everything off.

If you have trouble fitting in meditation or other rituals in the morning, try waking up just a little bit earlier. My meditation teacher says that people think they can't wake up earlier because they'll be sleepy, but meditation gives you energy. If you get up just twenty minutes earlier and meditate, you will actually have more energy than if you'd slept that extra time. Plus, you'll have all the other benefits, so it can be worthwhile to give it a try.

Take a Moment

What appealed to you in this chapter?
What didn't appeal to you?
Did this chapter spark any ideas for you?

17

Lezlie Laws

LEZLIE IS A certified Astanga yoga instructor, creativity coach, and owner of LifeArt Studio, where she guides people to make the life and the art they were born to create. She focuses on mind, body, and spirit and how they unite to create conscious living. Lezlie lives in Orlando, Florida.

"People who are living happy, meaningful lives create focused intentions, goals, and a mission. If you don't have a clear mission, a morning practice can give you the space to begin to figure it out."

I've done a morning practice for at least the past thirty years. I'm seventy now, and I started in my late thirties/early forties. When I started, it was not as extensive as what I do now because I was teaching and devoted to my career. I've been meditating even longer—for about fifty years. My morning practice is hugely important to me; it's responsible for the sense of joy and purpose I get to experience every day.

I'm an early bird, so I usually start at 5:30 a.m. Here's the routine:

1. Upon rising, I meditate for fifteen minutes.

2. I make a cup of Bulletproof coffee. (I live for this coffee. It's life-changing.)

3. I do my TIA Method journal. TIA stands for "thank," "intend," "ask." It's an expanded form of a gratitude journal, and it's pretty simple. I teach this practice to my clients and have recently put together a book that explains and supports this method:

    •   I make a list of experiences from the previous day for which I am grateful.

    •   I make a list of all the things I am intending to *be*, *do*, or *offer* throughout the day ahead of me.

    •   And finally, I ask my higher power (the universe, God, Source, Unity Consciousness, whatever you want to call it) to guide me in any issue or problem I'm grappling with.

I have filled dozens and dozens of spiral-bound sketchbooks with this morning gratitude routine over the years, and I credit this practice with giving me a sense of clarity, purpose, and joy in my life. Research has shown that the practice of gratitude really is the portal to cultivating these three qualities, just as all great wisdom traditions have told us for centuries.

4. After my journal writing comes thirty to sixty minutes of spiritual study and reading in the wisdom traditions.

5. I walk my dog, Dash. This has become our private walking meditation and sun salutation.

6. I head out to The Yoga Shala for eighty minutes of Astanga yoga.

Ahhhhhh. What a way to start the morning. I call it six steps to bliss. This way of starting the day sets me up to experience life in its fullness, to perform at my best, and to enjoy everything that comes my way. I find a morning ritual so essential to living fully that I require all of my clients to have one.

I was a writing teacher at Rollins College for forty-five years and quit teaching full-time four years ago. I've been a creativity coach for about six years. As I anticipated closing out my academic career and opening myself up to another one, I saw too many women my age who were completely lost. They were empty nesters or had failed marriages or were in jobs that had turned stale or uninspiring, and they just felt trapped. They would tell me, "I feel stuck, and I don't know why, and I don't know what to do."

It was sad to me. There is so much energy put toward helping college students find themselves, educate themselves, and prepare to do something meaningful in the world, yet there's this whole audience of older women—mainly baby boomers like me—who are struggling to create new meaning, and there's not much research on helping this population. Not only do they not know what to do, they often can't even articulate what they need.

I call myself a creativity coach because my plan was to work with this population, and the story I was hearing from these women was, "I've lost my creative mojo. When I was young I gardened, or I painted, or I made clothes, but I don't do that anymore." They had these creative outlets when they were younger, but somewhere along the line, their job, family, and household duties took over and they put their own creativity at the bottom of the list. Some felt shy about returning to their own creative work. They thought they were too late, or they didn't have enough time to get good at what they really wanted to do. I would say, "Who cares about being good! What about having fun?"

I came to see that these women weren't stuck as profoundly as they thought, and I could show them how to get unstuck—how to get out of the mindset that insists, "I can't do what I really want to do. I'm doomed because I'm older. It's too late for me."

The creative process fascinates me—what is it that makes some people embrace their creativity and other people think they're not creative? What are the conditions that people need to be creative? Research is filled with information on how to help ourselves out of a creative funk. It's wonderful to be able to share this with clients.

So that has become my job. I love finding out what makes someone's heart sing and then helping them discover that it's totally possible, and here's the way you do it. And the way you do it is to start with a morning practice! I call it a foundational practice, since to me it provides the foundation for living creatively.

As I listen to my clients, I see that when they feel stuck or like there are obstacles in their path, the true obstacle is that they haven't created a life structure that is spacious enough to allow them to realize their potential. And with just a little attention, time, and energy, that potential can be realized. Those are the three big things that women need, but I find that it's a language many women haven't used to think about their situation. Once that language is presented to them, they don't even really know what to do with it. I have to keep backing up—it's like in functional medicine where you're looking for the root cause of the symptom. I want to get at the root cause of what keeps them from giving attention, time, and energy to themselves.

I often find there are mental obstacles, such as the concept of "I don't have enough time because I have to work, come home, and cook dinner" and other limiting thoughts. They have patterns of living that they think are locked down: "This is how it's going to be for the rest of my life." And I see certain habits of mind these women hold that are literally keeping them from giving attention, time, and energy to the things they really want to do. Therefore, structures of living and habits of mind have become the two main pillars of my protocol.

I realized early on that the best thing they could do to hone the skills of attention, time, and energy was to undertake a foundational practice. I do a workshop on it that all my clients are required to take; that's how important I think a morning ritual is.

I get pushback from some people about doing their practice in the morning, but the research says it's most effective first thing upon waking. You're inclining your body, mind, and spirit toward the intentionality you want to bring to your day. However, I don't discourage clients if they need to do it at another time. I just think the morning is best. Do it when you can! It's better to do something at night than not at all.

Why a morning ritual is valuable to me

My morning practice has evolved over time, but it really is the foundation of my life. It connects me to Spirit, to my body, and to my intellectual life, as I incorporate prayer, meditation, yoga, reading, and writing. I'm lucky I can do it all in the morning now. At this point in my life, I'm retired and I live alone, so it's easy for me to create the schedule I want. When I was younger, married with a stepdaughter, and working, I didn't have that luxury. My practice wasn't as extensive, and I had to fit it in at various times throughout the day.

When I was building my career, I worked like a maniac. In my fifties, I started undoing all the bad habits that went along with my belief that overwork was a marker of success. I loved my work, but I exhausted myself. Now, my morning practice keeps me from overextending myself. I know I'm not giving my best if I'm overworking.

If we just focus on high performance and don't also focus on self-care, we will wear ourselves out. High performance needs to be balanced with a high degree of self-care, and I consider a foundational practice to be an essential form of self-care. It creates the conditions within me that allow me to offer my best to whomever or whatever I'm addressing throughout the rest of my day.

One of the things I teach in my workshop is that a foundational practice is something we do every single day that we know is going to allow us to perform at our very best twenty-four hours later. What we do today creates the path we will walk on tomorrow.

My suggestions for you

Look at this idea of a morning ritual as a life experiment. Think of yourself as a walking laboratory. Just like a scientist, be vigilant and observant about the way you're feeling and the way you're responding, and begin to connect how you feel with what you're doing in your morning practice.

Often, people don't realize that what they do in the morning affects the rest of their day. Bring attention to it and feel it in your body at a sensory level. You'll begin to notice that what you're doing in the morning is making your day go more smoothly, energizing you, and helping you perform better. As you see the results of the efforts you're putting in and realize how good it makes you feel, the habit gets installed because you know you'll get that feel-good payoff.

What practices should you include? There are four foundational practices I advocate for my clients: (1) eat and hydrate well, (2) sleep well, (3) move, and (4) meditate or do some sort of reflective practice. If they want, they can add to that, but those are the four essentials.

Meditation is so valuable. The research is replete with evidence as to its numerous benefits—it can reduce cortisol and bring clarity, calm, ease, focus, energy, a sense of purpose, a sense of equanimity, and a sense of connectedness with something bigger and greater than ourselves.

People often say, "I can't meditate because my mind is too crazy." I say, "That's why you have to!" Everybody's mind is crazy. Everyone has a hard time at first. It does take time for the effects to manifest. It's not instantaneous; it requires delayed gratification. But it has amazing effects. I ask my clients to start with just two minutes twice a day—before you eat in the morning and before you eat in the evening. Then I work with them on different techniques—there are so many ways to meditate, and it's important to find the method that suits them.

I also tell my clients, "Don't just do the basic practices I recommend; also figure out what brings you joy." If you ask many sixty-year-old women what brings them joy, you'll often get a long hesitation. If you ask any six-year-old, you get an immediate answer. If you have to think about what brings you joy, it's a sign you need to pay more attention to yourself.

I've recently taken up painting again, after putting it aside fifty years ago. Now I'm giving myself permission to get back to it. I'm not good at all, but I love it. I'm having so much fun. One of my art teachers, Lynn Whipple, does some great online classes and has put together art practices that are purely for the purposes of imbuing joy. She creates an art journal as part of her morning ritual.

I have a client who has a gorgeous garden. Every morning she walks down one side and up the other barefoot. She does this three hundred and sixty-five days a year, regardless of the weather. It connects her to nature, which is very important to her, and her day goes better when she does that. She's observed that about herself. She's become a student of her own life, and she knows what will benefit her.

I also ask my clients to be held accountable for their practice. When you're trying to implement a new habit, if you have an accountability partner, you will be more successful. Measuring it is also important. Keep a daily record of what you're doing, like a checklist.

Something that can help you get started with a practice is to begin to get in touch with what you feel, and connect those feelings with your actions. Catch yourself when you feel joyful; make a note of what's happening that's making you feel joyful. Put it in your journal. When you feel energized, look at what you've been doing and what you've been eating. Realize the connection between your actions and their effects. I have my clients make a list of the ten primary feelings they want to embody in their life. Then we examine everything they do and see how those actions connect to those feelings.

Find out what really works for you. Do you want to read a chapter of the _Tao Te Ching_? Walk your dog? Do breathing? What is it that settles you and grounds you? What opens you up? What allows you to be more aware, perceptive, loving, kind, and energized? What supports you in accomplishing your true mission?

I believe your practices should connect you to your mission. If you want your life to be more than okay—if you want it to be extraordinary, and to fulfill your potential—you have to have a mission. People who are living happy, meaningful lives create focused intentions, goals, and a mission. If you don't have a clear mission, a morning practice can give you the space to begin to figure it out.

Once you have established foundational practices, you have the space to get in touch with yourself and figure out what you want. When you are really clear about what your mission is, you don't want to fail at it, so you are motivated to do the practices that support it. Think about your eighty-year-old self. If you fail in your mission, how will she feel about that? That's motivating! That can keep you committed. I want to be a vitality-filled ninety-year-old, so I'm on the yoga mat every day, I don't eat sugar, and I surround myself with strong, uplifting people. I do my practices because I know they will keep me happy and vibrant, hopefully for the next twenty years!

It's helpful to spend time in the presence of others who have a successful morning practice. I hold creative momentum gatherings for the people I work with, and when new clients see how much the others are flourishing—how much their practice benefits them—they say, "I want that!" It really helps to be around others who are doing well; their joy rubs off on you.

Above all, focus on constructing a lifestyle that allows you to live consciously with full-out awareness and intention. Create a morning ritual that supports that lifestyle. Your ritual should be directly linked to the experience you want to have in your mind, body, and spirit. Make it positive: you should want to do your practice because it makes you feel good each day.

Take a Moment

What appealed to you in this chapter?
What didn't appeal to you?
Did this chapter spark any ideas for you?

18

Karen "KJ Sassypants" Hawkwood

KJ IS AN author and a Martha Beck Certified Master Life Coach who uses various tools, including astrology and self-assessments, to help clients achieve deep clarity about who they are and what they want. She lives in Boulder, Colorado.

"A morning ritual is about connecting with a deeper knowing of what is the right thing to do. Not what you can do, not how to do more, but what is the 'right action,' as they say in Buddhism. And it may be that the right action is no action."

I'm not a morning person. I've never been a morning person. When I was five years old I wasn't a morning person. It's not good if I get up and go straight into anything interactive, like talking to people or taking in information.

I have to respect the way in which I'm made. I use a great tool in my work with clients called Kolbe Indexes, which are self-assessments. One I use a lot is the Kolbe A Index. It measures a person's instinctive way of doing things and helps them understand how they can best use their natural strengths. For instance, I'm a fact finder, so I'm always seeking information. Trying to pretend I'm not a fact finder will just make me frustrated.

My cell phone is my morning alarm. My tendency used to be that I'd grab it first thing and look at the news. That was a very detrimental thing to do to myself. So I found a really cool app called Flipboard that allows you to curate a wide array of topics. Now when I look at my phone in the morning, it's not headline news. It's fun, interesting, encouraging information—and that's actually good for me. It wakes up my mind and gets me curious and thinking.

I usually get up somewhere between 8:00 and 10:00 a.m. and make my coffee. Even if I've had a good sleep, the coffee is usually necessary. I'd love to believe I could one day adjust my physicality to the point where I can be bright-eyed and bushy-tailed without any caffeine, but until that day comes, I make my coffee.

There is a certain sequence and physical ritual to making coffee that I like. I use a type of French press called an Aeropress. It's a little cylinder, and you grind the coffee, put it in, put the boiling water in, and then press the coffee right through. It makes excellent coffee. As I'm doing that, I'm looking through my Flipboard at articles on solar energy, new neuroscience findings, or interesting information on aging—all sorts of stuff. I have a wide range of interests. Between the coffee and the Flipboard, that's how I fully wake up.

Then I do something that's very important to me—I go and sit at my ancestors' shrine. This is part of my spiritual work. I just started doing it a few years ago, but it has become the most comforting thing for me. It's a time of self-reflection because I actually talk to them. I sit in front of this shelf full of candles, stone statues, pictures of my people who have passed on, and all kinds of different symbols, and I talk to them out loud. If I'm feeling great I tell them; if I'm having a rough day I tell them. And they listen.

If I need help I ask for it, which is something that has been super hard for me. I grew up an only child and very isolated. I went to eight schools in twelve years, and I got used to not having anybody to ask. So learning to do that each morning has been really meaningful. If I'm feeling off-kilter and I ask them for help, I might not always get a detailed response, but I usually feel their attention and that makes me feel better. Also, I'll kind of figure myself out. It's similar to the function journaling plays for a lot of people, where you write it down and then you realize, "Oh, that's what's going on."

I always light a candle. Sometimes I will offer my ancestors a piece of fruit, some cool water, or another kind of gift. Often I will make them coffee too. It sounds a little absurd, but after a couple of years, I've gotten pretty used to it.

Those are the parts of my ritual that are quite consistent. There are a few others that rotate in and out. A lot of the practices I have come from a teacher whose work I followed fairly intensely for the last few years. His premise is that we all have a dimension that is what he calls the "best of us." It's the biggest, wisest, most powerful, and most loving part of us. Then on the other end of the scale, we have what he calls our "smallness."

It's all the yucky stuff, and what's interesting is that a lot of it isn't even real.

There are questions you can ask to get in touch with your best side: What does it look like? What does it feel like? What kind of music does it like? What colors does it like? Once you know the answers to those questions, you can surround yourself with those things. I like this because it gives me tangible actions even though it's essentially a deeply psycho-spiritual approach. It's an interesting perspective because a lot of approaches to spirituality are almost exclusively inner focused. That's never worked for me. I need to combine the spiritual and the physical.

My focus these days is on intentionally opening the channel to that best part of me. I have carefully chosen images on my walls. I have music that evokes that part of me. I have special pieces of jewelry. And I have these incredible essential oils and flower essence blends. I use some or all of those during my morning ritual to connect with myself.

Sitting in stillness is a practice that I find serves me better the more I do it. But it's an area where my morning ritual is a work in progress; I'm still trying to figure out the order. If I try to sit when I first wake up, I'm too sleepy. Stillness requires a certain amount of actually being awake, weirdly. But once I've been reading my interesting material and drinking my coffee, my mind is often too revved up, and then it's hard to do. Plus, after I've had my coffee, read my stuff, and talked to my people, I've used up all the time that I have. So I'm trying to figure out how to fit it in each day, because sitting in stillness is supposed to be *the* thing. This is the practice that pretty much everyone agrees on, and when I do it, it benefits me.

It's not about trying to make the mind stop. I know better. The mind doesn't stop. Learning that was important because I believed that stillness was about having the mind not produce any thoughts. I don't know, maybe that happens for the Dalai Lama, but aspiring to that is just going to make me feel bad. For me, it's about letting the mind burble and not paying attention to it. That is hard, but it's way more doable than trying to actually silence the thoughts.

What often happens that makes me not want to sit is that I come face-to-face with myself. Sometimes painful stuff will come up, and I don't want to deal with it. Of course that doesn't mean it's not there. Ignoring the elephant does not make it go away. And this is actually precisely why sitting in stillness is something I should be doing more often. It's definitely something I'm working on.

When I travel, I take a few simple elements of my shrine with me as a kind of anchor point. The physical location of the shrine—or of any church, mosque, or temple—doesn't matter. The place itself isn't the magic. It doesn't allow or prevent connection with the divine, it just makes it easier. When I travel and take a few pieces that act as points of connection, it's like a "shrine lite." It serves the same function and I do exactly the same thing. I will do that pretty much without fail every day when I'm not at home.

Why a morning ritual is valuable to me

When I talk to my ancestors in the morning, it really makes a difference—especially if I'm feeling rocky. If I'm feeling off, the odds are good that the "smaller" part of my being has grabbed the wheel, as it does. When that happens, my teacher recommends not to fight it. Instead, I pay attention to the better part of myself. My ritual gives me physical ways to connect with that part, and it really helps.

On the days that I'm not able to do a full ritual, just a quick "Hey, love you, bye" to my ancestors, I feel scattered. My days feel like when you lean too far over and you have to run to keep from falling. I'm behind, and there's a frantic quality to everything I do. I don't have that sense of connection with the core of me that knows what to do. I don't feel like I have any space in myself or in my day. Even if I have an open calendar, I'll still feel like that, which shows how absurdly perceptual the whole thing is.

When I feel that way, I don't make good decisions. Even if it's as simple as whether to have a cup of tea or not, I'm deciding from a hurried, distracted place because my mind is anywhere but right here. I'm processing forty-seven other things while I'm trying to decide whether to have a cup of tea. Nothing good comes of that state.

When I take the time and give my rituals deliberate attention, I engage not just with myself but with the best of me—my wisest self. When I do that, the house could be burning down and I would still feel centered and able to work in a way that is effective and powerful but not frantic.

It's very beneficial to take the time to do my ritual each day. I'm learning just how important it is. But I have a hard time keeping it up consistently because of my nature; I'm what I call a race horse rather than a plough horse. I tend to do a bunch of things in one big rush and then rest—or collapse, depending on your perspective. As much as I would love to be a plough horse person who can be steady and consistent, that's not me. I have fought myself on that for thirty years (I just turned fifty) and haven't been able to turn myself into a plough horse yet. Now I'm finally thinking, "Okay, how do I live life as a race horse?"

When I'm in a phase where I get excited and want to do "all the things," I stay up too late. When I stay up too late, then I sleep later and that costs me the morning. I need to learn how to balance my race horse nature with being able to do a full morning ritual. That continues to be an ongoing challenge for me.

Ritual has to have a purpose or it's just mechanical. The most powerful purpose a morning ritual has is to connect us with who we really are, at our deepest and at our best. It centers us and settles us. It gets our wheel on the track of where we really want to go.

When we connect with the truest part of ourselves, we know what it is we need. Some days that might be going all out, jet thrusters to the max. Other days it might be saying, "My doing today is to be still." The best way a morning ritual can serve us is to help us know what is right for us in the moment.

My suggestions for you

If you tend to set your alarm so late that you barely have enough time to grab a protein bar on the way out of the door, consider getting up a little earlier. The trade-off between fifteen minutes of sleep and fifteen minutes of intentional engagement with yourself is so worth it. Getting fifteen fewer minutes of sleep is not a big deal—and if it is to you, consider that an emergency. That's a different situation and you need to focus on that. For most people, though, it's a worthwhile trade-off. I don't care what you do—just do something to connect with your best self. Take that fifteen minutes and protect that time.

I know most people feel like there isn't enough time in the day to do what we want. I love Jill Farmer's book, *There's Not Enough Time ... and Other Lies We Tell Ourselves*. She says that this belief is a complete fallacy. Every day, you have the same twenty-four hours you always do and that everyone else does. What you have to do is study how you allocate that time. What are you choosing to give your time to? I'm not saying you should ignore your children in the morning or wake up at 4:00 a.m. I couldn't get up at 4:00 a.m. if my life depended on it. If somebody guaranteed me enlightenment, I couldn't do it. But if you pay close attention to your schedule, you can probably identify some ways to create a pocket of time for yourself.

If I was coaching you, I would ask you to examine your "should." What do you think you *should* be doing with your time? There's a quote I use with my clients a lot: "If you want something you've never had, you have to do something you've never done." I think we want to feel the peace and centeredness that comes with a morning ritual. We want to feel all of a piece instead of scattered over five counties, but we feel scattered over five counties because of the way we're currently choosing to live. We have to make different choices if we want to feel differently.

I don't care if your ritual happens first thing in the morning, although I think it does make a bigger difference to your day if it does. But just take fifteen minutes that are completely protected, where you aren't doing anything else. Then do whatever feels good in that time. Sit in stillness if you can manage it. Look at something beautiful, whether that's your garden, your dog, or a picture of the place you want to visit—anything that invites you into a peaceful, expansive state. Just do that and then build on it. That isn't impossible for anybody. If you can do that in the morning and set the energetic ground of your day, it really has a positive impact on how your day goes.

If I were to suggest a specific practice, I would advocate sitting in stillness if you can. If you find it challenging because it makes you confront things in a way that you're not ready for, then you can try a simple technique my teacher recommends. He says that what is in our environment affects how we feel. This isn't an idea that's unique to him; you can find it in Marie Kondo's book *The Life-Changing Magic of Tidying Up* or in the principles of the Chinese practice of feng shui, which goes back thousands of years.

Pay attention to how the things in your world make you feel, and if something doesn't make you feel good, get rid of it. As Marie Kondo says, if an item doesn't spark joy, let it go.

Find an object, an image, or a piece of music that makes you feel amazing—something you already have, so you don't have to go buy anything. Hold that item, look at that picture, or play that music and feel how it connects you to the best part of yourself.

My teacher talks all the time about how clothes affect us. I used to roll my eyes at that, until I started paying attention to how I felt when I wore certain things. I will never again own a pair of plain flats. They make me feel like the most drab, boring, conventional, uninteresting human being, and that's not who I am. It may sound like a silly idea, but it's actually very powerful.

What is your favorite piece of clothing? Maybe it's a dress you wore to a wonderful party. Maybe it's your wedding dress. Maybe it's your overalls because you wear them to work on your land and that makes you feel glorious. Whatever it is, picture it.

You don't have to put it on, but you can sit and imagine yourself wearing it. That's all. Just do a couple minutes of that. Or maybe there is a piece of music that makes you feel incredible. I love Sara Bareilles's song "Brave." When I listen to that song, I cannot feel more awesome. Listen to something you love, or just imagine it in your head. That's all it takes.

It's important to not use a morning ritual as a productivity hack. We can get caught in that trap of always doing. We don't need to do more, more, more, especially if what we're doing isn't good for us. We have done ourselves almost to death with that energy in our culture for hundreds of years. My personal perspective is that we are now seeing the result of that in our world, and we need to question that way of being.

A morning ritual is about connecting with a deeper knowing of what is the right thing to do. Not what you *can* do, not how to do more, but what is the "right action," as they say in Buddhism. And it may be that the right action is no action. You may need to slow down and come from the place that has no fear so you can see what to do. If you can set aside your fear—not dismiss it, not act like it isn't there, not shame it or punish it or struggle with it but simply set it to one side—then you can see what else is there. It's the most life-changing thing I ever learned, and a morning ritual provides space for you to do that.

Let's talk more about fear for a moment. It tends to drive so much of our behavior, and yet there's this idea that we shouldn't have fear. I think we have to learn to do what we can, with what we have, where we are. Most of us still have a very active amygdala, which is the older, instinctive part of the brain where the fight-or-flight response originates. We can acknowledge that the fear we feel is usually not helpful, that it's an evolutionary reflex that isn't useful in the absence of a legitimate threat, and that it's not going away. Then we can look for what else is there alongside the fear, underneath the fear, behind the fear. If we don't try to suppress it but simply say, "Yes, yes, I see you—now I'm going to look for what else is here," that's when we find the interesting stuff.

This is where connecting with that best part of us is critical, because that part doesn't let fear make decisions. It doesn't let fear drive. That best part of us drives from love. To me, love isn't just squishy and sweet—it has teeth. Driving from love can be a very fierce and intense process. It doesn't always feel good, but it's a whole different story than letting fear drive.

It's important to pause enough to find that place where we can cast an eye over ourselves and ask, "What state am I in, and who is in the driver's seat right now?" If you do that and see that fear is driving, and you put somebody else in the driver's seat, you're going to have a radically different day. By doing that every day, by just stopping and saying, "Hey, what's going on with me? Where am I? Who's driving?" you are strengthening a necessary muscle. You are developing the part of you that knows how to have that discernment and be able to see what is really going on, and put love into the driver's seat rather than fear. Any type of morning practice that directs you more toward that centered, grounded, powerful love inside of you is incredibly valuable.

As you decide what to do for your morning ritual, be wary of extreme solutions (like waking up at 4:00 a.m. or running ten miles every single day). We in America tend to love extremity, but it's not sustainable. Choose something that you can keep going.

Lastly, it's important to stay fluid. Know when your practice needs to change. It's very easy to get habitual, and when we fall into that, there's no juice anymore. We're just doing something because that's what we do; it's no longer serving us. Cultivate an awareness of what you're doing and regularly check in to see if your practice is achieving what you need it to. To me, that is as important as having a practice in the first place.

Take a Moment

What appealed to you in this chapter?
What didn't appeal to you?
Did this chapter spark any ideas for you?

19

Koelle Simpson

KOELLE IS A world-renowned life coach, horse whisperer, and leader of the Equus Coaching Movement, which helps people reconnect with their true nature via transformative experiences with horses. She is currently traveling the world to share her work.

"Creating the space to connect with ourselves is about getting in touch with what our genuine needs are, and what we need to feel more alive. … Sometimes what we need could be just five minutes of sitting in bed before we do anything, and that can be a powerful morning practice."

Creating some kind of a morning ritual is incredibly grounding. My needs and the practices I use have changed at different times in my life. For the last couple of years, I've been doing breathwork and Qi Gong as a way to settle into connecting with myself. They slowly bring me awake and help me start in the energy state I want to be in for the day. [Author's note: this spelling of Qi Gong is Koelle's preference; it can also be spelled Chi Kung.]

My ritual helps me transition from the dream state. Since my ritual occurs at a time when my different layers of consciousness are more blended, it's a little easier to be aware of things that might be going on mentally, psychologically, and emotionally. That awareness maybe wouldn't be as easy to access if I was trying to do it later in the day.

I like to wake up early enough that I don't feel time pressure. My wake-up time varies a lot, since each day is completely different for me. I wouldn't suggest this for everyone; I think a consistent routine can be helpful. But I have made a conscious choice to keep traveling and sharing my work right now, so my schedule changes every day. Because I ask a lot of my body with all the travel, I nourish it with plenty of quality sleep, diet, and exercise, and also the emotional fulfillment that comes from connecting with incredible people and doing work that's really meaningful to me.

I travel all over the world and am often in radically different time zones. When I first get to an international location, I'll usually skip my practice the first day or two so I can focus on getting enough sleep. My morning practice happens about ninety-five percent of the time, and then there's that five percent when it's just not practical and I need to sleep.

I think I've lost track of whatever my natural inclination would be in terms of getting up, but I do okay with waking up early and getting the day moving. However, I prefer to be quiet when I first wake up. I don't like to do a lot of talking or discussing. I'm not very social first thing. I'm not the person who comes bounding out of bed. I like to make that transition a lot more slowly.

Once I wake up, while I'm still in bed, I become aware of my breath. I start with a very slow in-breath and out-breath. Then I sit up and begin to breathe in to the top of capacity and hold, then breathe out all the oxygen and hold for a few seconds. I visualize the qi (life force) that moves through our energy centers, flowing through our bodies in a serpentine or spiral movement. I envision the masculine and feminine sides of my persona, and the ways those work together to develop my character, weaving back and forth through my body and up my spine to the top of my head. As I breathe in air, I draw that visualization up all the way to the top of the head, and then I circulate that energy into my brain so that I begin to create more awareness, alertness, and self-compassion. As I breathe out, I imagine the same energy coming down the front of my body, creating a circular loop.

I usually do this for about ten minutes. There's no rigidity about it. I let my body tell me when it feels energized or when I need to slow down and put my attention in a place where I feel blockage or resistance.

After a few rounds of that, I will do the yogic breath of fire, where you contract your diaphragm firmly and breathe in and out through the nose in rapid succession. Then I'll get up and do a little bit of stretching the areas that feel stiff—anywhere my body is asking for attention.

Next, I begin the Qi Gong practice. I usually do it in whatever room I happen to be in, but if I have the opportunity, I will take go outside. It would be a wonderful gift to be able to do a regular practice with a community or a master, but given my travel schedule, it's not realistic at this point. I get the information that I need online and do it on my own. I let my body show me what it needs.

Qi Gong is an incredibly good practice for getting in touch with the way energy flows through the body. As I start to oxygenate my blood and get things circulating, I become aware of the subtleties of my frame and my positioning—what I'm doing and how I'm doing it.

It also connects me more to an emotional awareness. That is really important because in order to have a choice about what we're bringing to our day and how we're choosing to show up in the world—what aspects of ourselves we want to bring into the foreground and what aspects of ourselves we want to give less attention to—it's important to know what our emotional states are. Then we can get in touch with our genuine needs, not just an ideal about where we think we should be.

I have tried doing a sitting meditation practice, but it wasn't a great fit for me; it didn't bring me the level of movement I needed to connect to myself. Currently, breathwork and Qi Gong serve as meditation for me.

I used to do a walking meditation with my yellow Lab, Cole. Then, during the last couple of years of his life, he was completely blind and couldn't go for walks anymore. I would go into a fenced pasture with him and just witness him exploring the world without sight. We would spend about forty-five minutes being together, and that was a really profound meditation. It would bring me into awareness, as I would start to think, "Oh, I have to get back now." Then I would question, "Get back to what, and why? Is this feeling something that I want to keep bringing to life? Or do I want to choose something different?" It's looking at life as being about accomplishing a task versus "What is the experience I want to be having in this moment?"

This awareness can put us in connection with the reality of our own death, which is something we all need but that we tend to avoid. When we're aware of that, we engage more in the conscious choosing of the experience we want to have each moment and each day.

I consider life itself a meditation. I don't believe in the idea that we need to stop thinking when we meditate. We need stories to bond to life; we live stories. The question is, which story are we choosing to live by? We've had a lot of stories given to us by our culture—rules and ideas about what is good and what is not good—many of which we're not even conscious of playing out. To me, meditation is any time we're doing something that supports self-awareness, where we become conscious of what stories we're bonding to.

When we are conscious of that, we give ourselves access to choice. I think that's one of the reasons why Byron Katie's work is so powerful—she has helped people recognize that we're telling stories about our experiences and we can question those stories. There is no absolute truth. It's all relational truth. We get to choose. We don't have to deny what has happened and how it has caused us to feel—we can honor our emotions about it—but at the same time, we can choose the meaning we create from the experience we're having.

To me, meditation is that; it's an experience of self-awareness. I may not be awake to it all the time, but every moment of life is inviting me into more self-awareness. Every moment of life is a fractal expression of the relationship we're having with ourselves.

Why a morning ritual is valuable to me

Part of the reason I've been drawn to breathwork and Qi Gong is because I'm starting to come into a more intimate connection with the life force energy that moves through all things. When I was younger, and even when I was first starting my business, I took it for granted. I used my will to push through and persevere, regardless of what my body or emotions were saying. I've realized how incredibly counterproductive that is, both for the work I want to do and for the enjoyment of my own experience of being alive.

Learning to cultivate an awareness of and genuine relationship to that life force energy has been a spiritual experience and a game changer for me. It gives me a much stronger connection to my own desire—to my awareness of what I want to bring to life. I love the quote from Shakespeare, "All the world's a stage, and all the men and women merely players." It's such a fantastic quote because we are not here to get to some finite accomplishment. Rather, the point of life is to collect experiences—and that doesn't mean avoiding uncomfortable ones and only having nice ones! Every living thing goes through natural cycles of change, and that includes a lot of challenge. But it also includes the incredible life force energy that happens in the spring, the maturity that happens in the summer, the collection of abundance that happens in the fall, and then everything going dark and dissolving in the winter.

We all go through these cycles. Our ability to be more in touch with how the life force energy moves through us and all things gives us the opportunity to have more choice—more choice about where we put our attention, where we cultivate that energy, and what we want to create with it.

Where do we want to grow? What kind of personas and characters do we want to bring to life? Not coming from a place of fear about "This is who I need to be to belong or be loved or be accepted," but to come into a knowing that we can never not belong or not be loved. To come into a different understanding of life and suddenly have that deeper sense of safety and well-being that gives us access to an incredible amount of choice about how we want to show up in the world.

A morning ritual has changed a lot about my experience of life; it helps me recognize where I'm adopting the rules that have been given to me through culture so I can return to the freedom that we all actually have and be more conscious about what I choose to do.

My suggestions for you

Start listening to what your needs might be. Often we look at something like this and we think about it in terms of the ideal, like there's one thing we're supposed to do. I think it's more important to learn to listen to what your own needs are.

When we begin to meet our needs, the practice becomes something that's essential, like drinking water. We all want to drink water. We wouldn't go through an entire day without drinking water—otherwise, we'd be uncomfortable. Creating the space to connect with ourselves is about getting in touch with what our genuine needs are, and what we need to feel more alive. Any time we get still and ask ourselves that question with true openness for the answer, our minds, hearts, and psyches will slowly and gently guide us in that direction. Sometimes what we need could be just five minutes of sitting in bed before we do anything, and that can be a powerful morning practice.

I would encourage you not to idealize someone else's practice, but rather ask yourself with open curiosity about what you need to feel more connected to yourself, and utilize that for the time being until the answer to the question shifts to something else.

TAKE A MOMENT

What appealed to you in this chapter?
What didn't appeal to you?
Did this chapter spark any ideas for you?

20

Ashley Ellington Brown

I HAVE BEEN A freelance writer, primarily focusing on marketing and PR, since 2000. I also handle marketing and office management for my husband's music school, and we homeschool our son. We live in Florida.

"When I'm on vacation at the beach, I love to sit on the condo balcony each morning, drinking my coffee and watching the waves. My mind is peaceful; I have no worries or concerns because I'm on vacation! The day stretches ahead, wide open and full of possibility. When I'm at home, I can re-create that feeling with my morning ritual. For a little while I can press PAUSE on my brain and pretend I don't have anything to do."

I've never been a morning person, but implementing a morning ritual has truly changed my life. For example, last Saturday morning I looked at the clock and it was 8:15. I had already written my morning pages, stretched, walked the dog, made breakfast for my son, and fixed my coffee—and I felt good. I wasn't sleepy or grumpy! That is nothing short of a miracle, let me tell you. It's finally not torture for me to be up and about before 9:00 a.m. I'm proud of myself for creating this shift.

I've always loved to sleep, and I've tended to need a lot of sleep. When I was a baby, my mother often had to wake me up. I regularly slept until noon on weekends, even into my early thirties! Once I had my son—who did *not* like to sleep—that all came to a screeching halt. I was so sleep deprived that first year, I felt like a completely different person. My sweet husband, who is an early riser, began to get up with our son when he would wake at 4:00 or 5:00 a.m. so I could stay in bed—and I basically spent the next ten years trying to fill that sleep deficit. I jealously guarded my sleep like a thief hoards jewels.

But last year I became aware that I felt tired every day, even when I got nine or ten hours of sleep. I also was irritable much too often. I researched possible causes for this and discovered that my nightly glass of wine could be adversely affecting my sleep quality. I started skipping it—and what do you know? I began to feel somewhat more rested and less grumpy.

I also took a hard look at my mornings. I was hitting the SNOOZE button until I absolutely had to get up, then jumping out of bed with that adrenalized feeling of being late. I would stumble to the kitchen feeling groggy and race around doing chores while I gulped my coffee. It was an awful way to start the day—no wonder I didn't want to get up! No wonder I was irritable! I decided to stop hitting SNOOZE. Rather, I would open my eyes and lie in bed for a moment, stretching and breathing deeply—and consciously *not* thinking about my to-do list.

As I did this for a few weeks, I began to feel much more in control and relaxed in the mornings, and that feeling would often last throughout the day. I started noticing that I was awakening around 7:00 or 7:30 a.m., then making myself go back to sleep if it wasn't yet officially time to get up. I decided to try getting up whenever I first awoke, just to see how I felt. I was amazed to find that I wasn't tired at all; as long as I was asleep by 11:00 p.m. I would wake up naturally around 7:00 or so and have plenty of energy all day.

I got into a rhythm of getting up on my own, before my alarm clock. It gave me more time in the mornings, which I decided to spend on myself. I would stay in the bedroom and journal or try to sit in silence—and it made me so happy! I realized I was creating a sort of morning ritual that was helping to put me in a positive frame of mind. I began to expand what I was doing, adding various practices I learned about, until I created my current ritual.

Now, after I wake up, I stay in bed for a few minutes and stretch. I hug my knees into my chest and say silently, "Peace to my left, peace to my right; peace behind me, peace in front of me; peace below me, peace above me; peace all around me; peace within me; peace to everyone." I breathe deeply a few times, then get up. I always keep a glass of water on my bedside table, and I'll drink about half of it to rehydrate. I dress in comfy clothes, brush my teeth, and splash my face to feel more alert.

In our bedroom there is a window that faces north and one that faces east, so I greet the directions as I raise the blinds. I learned about this practice in a class taught by life coaches

Wendy Battino (chapter 14) and Carla Robertson (chapter 1). I start with north, then go to the east-facing window. Then I turn to the south and the west, saying hello to each direction.

I sit in a chair in the corner of the bedroom and write morning pages (three pages of stream-of-consciousness writing by hand, as recommended in *The Artist's Way* by Julia Cameron). Next, I read a series of affirmations, some of which I wrote after thinking about what I want my life to look like (I've included a few samples in appendix 6), and some about creativity, which I got from *The Artist's Way*.

After that, I pull out my yoga mat and do some stretches on the floor. My lower back is stiff and achy in the morning, and this really helps it loosen up. I'll do cat/cow, child's pose, and downward dog. Then I lie on my back with my knees to my chest and roll side to side. I also love to do happy baby pose, where you lie on your back with knees bent and out to the side, bottoms of feet pointing at the sky, and hold your toes.

Next I try to sit in some sort of meditation for a few minutes. Sometimes I can, and sometimes I can't. It's hard for me to keep my mind quiet! Lately I've been focusing on a mantra while breathing in and out, and that seems to help. I want to expand this part of my practice in the future. After interviewing so many women who rave about the positive effects of meditation, I'd like to explore sitting for longer periods. After lunch most days I do a guided meditation, using the Abraham-Hicks Getting into the Vortex app, but I'm interested to see what effects a longer mindful meditation in the morning might have.

Except for when I'm writing morning pages—about what happened the day before, what I've got planned, or any fears or anxiety I'm feeling—I attempt to keep from thinking about what I need to do during the day. I try to leave all that on the page so I can be peaceful while I'm stretching and trying to meditate.

After stretching and sitting, I make the bed. It only takes a minute, but it really helps me feel more put together. If I skip this, I feel unsettled all day, especially when I go into the room and see the messy bed. It makes me feel like I don't have enough time to take care of the small things, which does not feel good.

Next, I go into the kitchen. My husband and son are usually already up and eating their breakfast. As I make toast or cereal for myself, I'll also give my son his allergy medicine and feed the dog. Then I fix my coffee and take it outside. Going outside is also something I learned about in the class with Wendy and Carla; it connects me to nature and makes me feel grounded. I stand in the grass facing the sun for a minute, then sit with my feet in the pool and watch the water ripple and swirl. I shush my mind and listen to the birds singing and the wind blowing through the trees. I soak up the sunshine and the glorious peace of nature, and let my thoughts float away on the clouds. I cradle the smooth warm mug in my hands and savor the rich flavor and aroma of my coffee. Occasionally, insights or ideas come to me during this time, as this book did.

Once I finish my coffee, I go inside and shower. The entire process takes about an hour and a half. Afterward, I'm ready to start the day's work. If I have an appointment first thing or a client needs my attention right away, I'll shorten the ritual or skip parts of it. On those days, though, I notice that I'm not nearly as centered or calm.

Why a morning ritual is valuable to me

When I'm on vacation at the beach, I love to sit on the condo balcony each morning, drinking my coffee and watching the waves. My mind is peaceful; I have no worries or concerns because I'm on vacation! The day stretches ahead, wide open and full of possibility. When I'm at home, I can re-create that feeling with my morning ritual. For a little while I can press PAUSE on my brain and pretend I don't have anything to do. I can enjoy the moment I'm in without worrying about what's to come. I feel spacious and free. It's like the quote from the 1980s movie *Earth Girls Are Easy*—I have a "mental margarita."

I used to wake up and immediately start thinking about my to-do list, which felt stressful and unpleasant. Now I use my morning ritual to center myself first, so that I'm able to think about my responsibilities more clearly and objectively.

Taking time for myself first thing in the morning also allows me to wake up fully before I see or speak to anyone else, which makes me a nicer person! I relish the peace it brings me and I'm grateful that I can start my day in this way. It's a far cry from when I had a corporate job and rolled out of bed bleary-eyed at 6:30 a.m., shoveling in cereal as I watched TV news and armored myself in suit, hose, and heels. Or from these most recent years when I would start each day deep in the mental muck. I have more patience now and feel out of control less often. I am happier and calmer, more centered and grounded, less frazzled and fearful.

Before I started making these changes, I felt like I had stopped growing as a person. I yearned for something more, but I was too sluggish to make anything happen. I craved a more creative life, engaged in projects that inspired me, but I couldn't clearly see what those might be. Then one day, sitting outside with my coffee, I had the idea for this book. Writing it has invigorated and expanded me beyond anything I dreamed of. Thank you, morning ritual!

My suggestions for you

It is so important to get enough rest before you try to make time for a morning ritual. I tend to need about nine hours, although occasionally I can manage on eight. That means I faithfully get in bed by 10:00 p.m. most nights, so I can be asleep by 11:00 and wake up at 7:00 a.m. The fact that I awaken on my own and don't feel tired later shows me that I'm getting enough rest. If you're trying to wake up earlier and find that you consistently need an alarm clock, you may not be sleeping enough. Being well rested is crucial for a happy life. Figure out how much is best for you, then do what you can to get it!

Once that's covered, start by taking a few minutes to wake up slowly while you're still in bed. Stretch a little and breathe deeply. Try to keep your thoughts away from anything stressful. Instead, remember your dreams from the night before, concentrate on your breathing, or make a mental list of what you're grateful for.

You might try doing a few stretches after you get out of bed. I've been amazed at how releasing the tension in my body seems to also relax my mind. It never occurred to be that I might be tense when I woke up. Often I don't even feel it, but once I'm on the mat I realize how tight I was. The movement loosens everything up and gets me in touch with my body.

If you can go for a walk in the morning, that will benefit both your body and your mind. Whenever I'm able to fit one in, I realize just how powerful it is. A walk energizes me physically and calms me mentally. I get into a rhythm of walking and breathing, and my thoughts slow down. I become more present as I pay attention to everything around me—the light shining through the leaves, the birds singing, the scent of pine needles, the squirrels dashing about. Walking never fails to lift my spirits.

When you don't have much time, take your morning coffee or tea somewhere peaceful—outside if you can, or to a part of your house where you can sit without being disturbed. Maybe you write while you sip; maybe you just watch the clouds. Whatever you do, make your morning ritual nourishing and enjoyable.

TAKE A MOMENT

What appealed to you in this chapter?
What didn't appeal to you?
Did this chapter spark any ideas for you?

21

Lagniappe: Extra Rituals

"LAGNIAPPE" MEANS "a little something extra." It's a popular word in New Orleans, where I grew up. Shopkeepers used to drop a small gift in the bag as a thank-you for customers and call it lagniappe. Now the term is used any time you get a little treat for free. So here: I'm handing you some extra morning rituals to savor!

Autumn Sanders, Creative Wellness Guide and Founder of MotherArts, New Jersey

A morning ritual—or process, as I have always called it—is essential. I have been doing morning pages from *The Artist's Way* for more than twenty years. I have boxes of notebooks! There are some gems in there that I am now culling to turn into a book. It's an amazing process of healing, discovery, and transformation.

Recently I have started to do a meditative drawing process. I draw for the length of a full CD or just a song, depending on how much time I have, and then I write down a few words that drop in. I always make myself (or my husband brings me) a cup of my favorite tea in a special mug before I begin.

When my kids were small, I did the five-minute version however and wherever I could—locked in the bathroom sometimes. And if I was running late and couldn't get to it first, I sat in the car for an extra few minutes after dropping them off at school. My morning process is nonnegotiable for me; it literally keeps me healthy, vital, and connected to my soul.

Katy Murray, Co-founder of Catalyst Collective, Lake District, United Kingdom

I get up thirty minutes before I wake my children up. I drink hot water with lemon, then do sun salutations and yoga stretches, focused breathing/meditation, and a gratitude/devotion/petition practice. If I have a bit more time, I'll fit in a five-minute high-energy workout, drink some green juice, and shower. Then I get the kids up, make them breakfast, take them to school … and the day rolls! And sometimes that all seems a bit much, and I enjoy some extra time in bed instead!

Claire Shamilla, Intuitive Energy Reader, New Zealand

I have a discipline of not checking social media in the mornings anymore and just allowing myself to enjoy the inner peace from a restful night's sleep. This has really helped shift my mornings, as I'm not thinking of all the things I have to get done. Instead,

I can be present with myself and the kids before they head off to school.

Emily Rosen Rittenberg, Coach and Owner at Nurture: Family Education and Guidance, Rochester, NY

I learned a lovely morning prayer when I was little. My son just learned it in Sunday school as a kindergartener. It's called "Modeh Ani," and you say it when you wake up. At the Jewish Community Center overnight camp I went to, we sang it around the flagpole before breakfast. The translation is: "I offer thanks to You, living and eternal King, for You have mercifully restored my soul within me. Your faithfulness is great."

Kim Blake, HR/Management Consultant for Start-ups, Canada

Morning pages from *The Artist's Way* have been transformative for me and the only morning habit I've been able to make stick. I've done them since September of 2015. I love that within the structure of writing three pages daily, there are no rules. I can write whatever I like, however I like.

Cheri Dostal Ryba, Women's Embodiment and Movement Educator, CIAYT, California

I have had lots of different morning rituals. Being a new mama means I am coming up with a new one each day. My primary goal for now is to check in with myself and adapt to the day. I am currently working on a basic dinacharya practice from

Ayurveda that includes splashing cool water on my face, tongue scraping after toothbrushing, and drinking warm tea. My movement practice feels all over the map, but it happens most days. My current meditation is a mantra practice while I nurse my daughter before bedtime. Adapt, flow, trust … all day long I'm practicing.

Cara Mendez, Spiritual Business Mentor for Homeschooling Mompreneurs, Missouri

I am a self-care advocate, recovering perfectionist, and home-schooling mom of five. I have found such grace in cultivating my morning self-care practice. I journal, practice pranayama breathing and yoga, and meditate. Occasionally, I use essential oils and crystals with my meditation. Once I complete this, I make a hot, healthy breakfast to nourish myself and my family.

Cristina Cho, CEO and Creative Director, Vixens Accessories, California

I used to struggle in the morning, always wanting to go back to sleep, then making eight cups of coffee for myself, then wanting to take a nap. Now I follow my daughter's lead. She wakes up in a great mood, ready to embrace the day with love and hope. She has completely changed the way I view mornings and helped me turn 180 degrees from the morning Eeyore that I was.

Alycia Buenger, Yoga Teacher and Writer, Ohio

I used to hate rituals (or at least that word and everything I felt about it), especially as a teenager. Now, since becoming a mother, morning and evening rituals are sacred times. It's incredibly complex to manage, because my mornings and evenings don't look the same every day.

My current morning routine includes waking up (alone—this, I've realized, is vital for me!), sometimes taking the pups outside for a short walk to check on the chickens and garden, and drinking warm water with lemon, all before my family wakes up. I'm working on incorporating some other elements, but am taking this one daily habit at a time.

Angela Winter, Voice and Creativity Coach, Virginia

Each morning I do morning pages and an energy work protocol that is akin to setting intentions and requesting help from the universe.

Beth LaGrone, Yoga Teacher, Massage Therapist, and Wellness Coach, Texas

My alarm is the Om Asatoma mantra ("Lead me from darkness to light," or from unconscious sleep to awake). Then I put on my morning mantra playlist and start a basic dinacharya practice: drinking warm water, body brushing, abhyanga self-massage, and some yoga asanas. Afterward, I shower, then do my morning meditation, draw angel and goddess cards, do my Money Love practices, and free write for about thirty minutes. Boom! Epic morning!

Mary Walker, Writer and Homeschooler, New Zealand

I homeschool our children, so my time alone is pretty much zero. Another homeschooling mum told me that she goes for an early morning walk before her husband leaves for work, and I realized I could do that too! So I don my walking shoes and head off down our country road. Initially, I could only manage twenty minutes because I had a knee injury. But it turns out, twenty minutes was all I needed to transform my day. The practice of walking seemed to open up my creativity. Daily, I would walk and lines of poems would start to fall from the sky, like strings of pearls. They would unfold as I walked, and I'd find myself repeating them, letting the rhythm of my footfall call more words forth. On the way home, I would repeat the lines to myself, editing and expanding as I went. When I got home, I would dash for a notebook and scribble down whatever I had, and that would be the start of my writing for the day.

The difference to my writing, my creativity—to what it feels like to start my day this way, on *my* terms, doing something only for me—is astounding. I've learned that it does not take as much time as I thought. Twenty minutes? That is a tiny investment with massive returns for me.

I've had other practices in the past. But with babies and small children, routines change so quickly. At times I've felt sad or hopeless about not being able to maintain mine. If I were to go back, I'd tell myself that *anything* I can do each morning is enough. That the *thing* might change, but the commitment to taking the time (even two minutes, leaning against the kitchen bench with a cup of tea alone) is like throwing open a window. And if we can stay flexible about what it is and what it looks like, we can begin to carve out more and more time for ourselves and recognize more easily what we need and want.

When we fall out of a routine, I think it would be great to have a thing to think or say or do that prevents us from feeling bad about ourselves. We need to give ourselves permission to deviate and permission to forget, understanding that in the end, nothing is lost by falling out of rhythm and then finding our way back in.

TAKE A MOMENT

What appealed to you in this chapter?
What didn't appeal to you?
Did this chapter spark any ideas for you?

22

Creating Your Own Beautiful Morning

A PERSONAL MORNING RITUAL will calm you, center you, and support you in creating a joyous, fulfilling life. As you reflect on what your own morning ritual might look like, consider the following guidelines and suggestions gathered from the previous chapters. You will also find a list of ideas in appendix 3, and some helpful tools in appendixes 2, 4, and 5.

Top ten takeaways

1. *Listen to yourself*

   Perhaps the most important message I got from all of these interviews is to be true to you. Respect your needs and the reality of your life and its ebbs and flows. A morning ritual is for you and you alone—it should nourish you, not be one more burden on your back.

   Do what makes you happy, what sparks you, what feels right for you. Ask yourself, "What do I need today?" Not

"What do I *have* to do?" or "What do others want me to do?" but "What do I need to do for me?"

2. ***Taking time for yourself = honoring yourself***

A morning ritual is an act of self-love. It's a way to cherish your one precious life. By paying attention to your inner voice, you're acknowledging that you matter. What you think matters. What you need matters. What you want matters. You are worthy of this attention, of taking the time to care for yourself and listen to yourself.

Your life is a miraculous gift. Imagine how you'd wash a delicate china teacup inherited from a beloved grandmother—carefully, gently, with reverence. You are infinitely more precious than any man-made object. Treat yourself with the reverence, care, and gentle tenderness that you deserve.

3. ***Your way is the right way for you***

Rituals are not one-size-fits-all. They are as individual as souls. Every woman in this book has a different approach that reflects her individual needs and preferences. Some women meditate, some don't. Some get up at dawn, while others couldn't do that if their lives depended on it. In other words, there is no right or wrong. Whatever works for you is right for you, regardless of what that is. Do what lights you up and feeds your unique soul.

The result is what counts, not the method. Decide how you want to feel, then choose the method that delivers that feeling for you. If you want to be calmer and meditation makes you calm, meditate. If meditation stresses you out, it's not the right method for you.

4. *Mindfulness is key*

When we're fully aware of the present moment, we can appreciate it. The ordinary becomes extraordinary. Our senses open up; the world is more vivid and delightful.

When we're completely present with others, our relationships improve dramatically. Our loved ones flourish in the warmth of our attention. We become closer, and that enhanced connection brings us joy.

5. *Sleep is vital*

If you're sleep deprived, a morning ritual isn't going to have much effect. Being well rested is the foundation for good health—both physical and mental. Ideally, you want to be able to wake up in the morning without an alarm—or at least not need to keep hitting SNOOZE.

If you're having trouble falling asleep, or get plenty of rest but still feel tired, try these tips:

i. Turn off all screens an hour before going to bed.

ii. Avoid alcohol and heavy meals in the evening.

iii. Do some calming stretches or take a warm bath.

iv. Write down whatever thoughts are swirling through your head.

v. Make sure your bedroom is cool and dark; ideally, it should also be free of electronic devices, like your phone.

vi. Try to get some sun first thing in the morning to reset your biological clock.

vii. Get some exercise each day.

6. *You don't have to get up at dawn*

   Few people can rise at dawn and still be well rested. If you can fit a ritual into your morning while getting enough sleep, that's marvelous. But if not, find the time that suits you best.

   If you feel like you can't find any time at all, track what you do for a day. See if there are any hidden timewasters, like social media, and create pockets where you can. If that doesn't work, check out the last tip under "Seven suggestions for crafting your ritual" at the end of this chapter.

7. *Start small*

   A short and consistent practice beats a long but infrequent one every time. Keep it simple and achievable. To help with consistency, attach it to an existing habit. For example, take your morning coffee or tea outside and sit in stillness while you drink it.

   Take it easy and make it easy. Start with tiny changes (i.e., I will take ten slow breaths in bed each morning this week), then add on as those become routine.

8. *Silence brings clarity*

   When we tune out distractions and listen to our inner voice, we discover what we need. Insights can come to us about issues we are facing.

   Silence and stillness give us space to dream. We can visualize what will make us happy, and we can see clearly how to achieve it.

9. *Be flexible*

   Life happens. Energy levels fluctuate. Schedules change. You change. If you find your ritual is no longer nourishing, modify it or create a completely new one. If you hit a rough patch, turn into the skid. Do what you can when you can. Focus on what will make you feel best each day—what do you need to get through that time in one piece?

Create a ritual that fits your life as it is. Perhaps you have small children or a busy work schedule and can't manage a full practice during the week. You could do something quick on weekday mornings, then have a longer ritual on weekends. Or you could create a ritual later in the day when you have more time, perhaps at lunch or in the evening.

10. *Be kind to yourself*

Don't beat yourself up if you miss a day or a week. Everyone goes through challenging periods. Even during calm times, it's difficult to change your habits. Treat yourself gently.

Avoid "compare and despair"—rather than looking at what others are doing, focus on your own path. If you are trying, you are succeeding. Every action counts, no matter how small. Hey, just making the time to read this book is an accomplishment!

Encourage yourself. Celebrate your achievements, no matter how ridiculously tiny they may seem. Give yourself treats. Be your own cheerleader. If you enjoy tracking your progress, make a calendar chart that you can check off (you might want to use some of those cute teacher stickers: "Great job!" "Way to go!" "You're a star!"). You can also use the Ritual Tracker form (in appendix 2 and available as a download at www.abeautifulmorningbook.com/resources).

Perhaps you would enjoy teaming up with others. I've created a closed Facebook group to provide a forum for sharing and support (see details in Closing Thoughts); you can join that, or seek out like-minded friends.

Seven suggestions for crafting your ritual

1. *Start your day with a positive mindset*

   The morning sets the tone for the day. Instead of looking at the news or checking email first thing, do something calming and uplifting. Make a list of what you're grateful for. Read something inspiring. Listen to music that evokes joy.

2. *Nature is a portal to peace*

   The natural world soothes us. We are animals, after all, and being outdoors feels … well, natural! Simply stepping outside can calm us down if we are stressed. We become grounded and centered. Our breathing slows as we unconsciously mirror the peaceful rhythms of nature. We are taken beyond ourselves as we pay attention to the sights, sounds, and scents around us. We are refreshed and rejuvenated. We realize the connection between us and every living thing. We feel comforted knowing that we are part of an infinite and glorious whole.

3. *Sitting in stillness centers us*

   We access our deepest selves when we get still and quiet. We become aware of how we are feeling, and what our inner voice is whispering.

   There are many ways to sit in stillness; you don't have to meditate in a lotus position for an hour. You can get comfortable in a chair and simply pay attention to your breath, or silently repeat a word or phrase (like "peace" or "All is well"). You can sit outside and lose yourself in nature. You don't even have to sit, actually. The rhythm of walking or a movement practice like yoga can lull your mind into that calm state.

4. *Movement benefits the body and mind*

Exercise invigorates you, not only physically but also mentally. It leaves you energized and enthusiastic and clears your mind. If you can incorporate some form of movement into your morning ritual, it will jumpstart your day.

5. *Gratitude attracts more reasons to be grateful*

When you start the day thinking about what's good in your life and feeling thankful for it, you clear the pathway for more good to come. Look for things to appreciate, and you will find more and more of them.

Gratitude is an easy practice. In any given moment, you can find something to be grateful for, and you can do this at any time. Think about the fact that you are breathing with no effort at all—what a miracle! Consider other ordinary events that we take for granted, like turning on a tap and getting hot water instantly, hugging a loved one, or laughing with a friend. Appreciate constants, like the sun: always rising, shining every day even when clouds block it from view, making our lives possible.

6. *Relaxing your body relaxes your mind*

We all hold tension in our bodies. Often we are unconsciously clenched and don't even realize it.

The next time you get upset, take a moment to scan your body and feel the physical effects of your thoughts and emotions. When you become present in your body, noticing where there is tightness, you give yourself the ability to fix it. When you stretch that area, you relax the body, and the mind follows. You can then think about what caused the tightness and make changes going forward to prevent it from occurring again.

Our muscles hold tension even while we sleep. Stretching as part of your morning ritual will release that tension and help you start the day in a calmer frame of mind.

7. *Mindfulness during daily activities is restorative*

You don't necessarily have to add anything to your day. If you can cultivate mindfulness as you go about your usual activities, it can have the same restorative effect as a morning ritual. Breathing deeply when you wake up, pausing to feel your feet on the floor before you get out of bed, paying attention to the sensation of warm water flowing over your skin in the shower, watching the clouds while sipping your coffee—these practices can all calm and center you, and they don't take any extra time.

Maybe being mindful during your day is all you can do right now. If you have young children or an overwhelming schedule, just take that time you already spend in the shower or eating breakfast or commuting to work, and make it yours. Quiet your thoughts by focusing on sensations: your breath as it passes your lips, the air or water on your skin, the sounds around you. Breathe slowly and deeply. Close your eyes if you can. Try saying a lovingkindness meditation: "May I be well. May I be happy. May I be filled with peace." Pray. Count your blessings. Sing your favorite song in your head. The point is to claim those minutes entirely for yourself, to nourish your soul and connect you to yourself. Even those tiny actions can have an enormous positive impact.

TAKE A MOMENT

What appealed to you in this chapter?
What didn't appeal to you?
Did this chapter spark any ideas for you?

Closing Thoughts

EACH WOMAN FEATURED in this book crafted her morning ritual over time, to suit her particular life and her particular personality. As you consider what you want yours to look like, be true to yourself. Be kind to yourself. The entire point of creating a morning ritual is to treat yourself well. It's not meant to be work or something you must strive toward. The path to peace does not go through Stressville. Be lighthearted and free. Experiment with a variety of ideas and see what makes you feel best.

Your ritual doesn't need to be elaborate, either. There is power in simplicity. A practice doesn't have to be complex to be meaningful and transformative. What tiny tweaks could you make to your current schedule or routine that might have a positive effect? What easy practice could you implement tomorrow? Start small and build from there.

You can do this! You don't need to be a life coach, a yoga instructor, or a Zen master. You already have what you need within you. Think about what resonated as you read. What called to you? If you took notes or marked certain sections, look back through those.

In the appendixes, you will find an abundance of resources to help you create your own morning ritual, including questions to contemplate and words to describe the life you want. The Resources section provides a reading list of books that will inspire you, as well as a list of links to additional information about practices and materials mentioned in the interviews. You can also access live links and downloadable files, including a Ritual Tracker form, at www.abeautifulmorningbook.com/resources.

I hope that reading this book has been an uplifting experience and that you have discovered ideas and insights that will enhance your life. I invite you to visit the book website for more ideas that can help you, as well as fun treats like pictures of the women featured in this book and their morning rituals.

If you would like to be part of the *Beautiful Morning* Community, a closed Facebook group where you can talk about your experiences, get support, and encourage others, just send me an email at Ashley@abeautifulmorningbook.com. You can also sign up for my mailing list at www.abeautifulmorningbook.com.

I would love to hear how it's going as you create your own ritual. Feel free to share on Facebook, either on the book page or in the group (social media links are on the book website).

Enjoy yourself as you create a future full of beautiful mornings and a gorgeous life overflowing with all that you desire!

Appendix 1
Permission Slip

Sometimes we can feel like we need official permission to do something for ourselves. If you feel this way, here it is! You have two choices: you can give yourself permission, or I can give it to you. Fill out whichever "permission slip" is most powerful for you. Make a copy and put it somewhere prominent, if you like, to remind you that you have the absolute right to do this for yourself.

You can also download these at
www.abeautifulmorningbook.com/resources.

I, _____, give myself permission to take time for myself each day to create a personal ritual and declare it as my sacred space, necessary to my well-being and protected from encroachment by others. I am allowed to do whatever feels right for me to create a beautiful, nourishing start to my day.

I am allowed to skip my morning ritual at any time, for any reason. I will take each day as it comes and treat myself with tender care, doing whatever is best for me at that time.

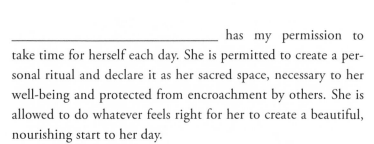

_____ has my permission to take time for herself each day. She is permitted to create a personal ritual and declare it as her sacred space, necessary to her well-being and protected from encroachment by others. She is allowed to do whatever feels right for her to create a beautiful, nourishing start to her day.

She is also allowed to skip her morning ritual at any time, for any reason. She has my permission to take each day as it comes and to treat herself with tender care, doing whatever is best for her at that time.

—Ashley Ellington Brown

Appendix 2
Morning Ritual Tracker

Monday ☐

_____

_____

Tuesday ☐

_____

_____

Wednesday ☐

_____

_____

Thursday ☐

_____

_____

Friday ☐

_____

_____

Saturday ☐

_____

_____

Sunday ☐

_____

_____

(You can find a customizable and printable form at
www.abeautifulmorningbook.com/resources.)

Appendix 3
Morning Ritual Ideas

- Gratitude practice: think about or write down what you're grateful for
- Sit outside
- Paint, draw, doodle, craft, scrapbook, knit, sew
- Say affirmations
- Visualize
- Set intentions
- Read
- Dream about what you want your life to look like
- Greet the four directions
- Think through your day and pick your top priority—what is the most important thing that you want/need to accomplish?

Meditate:

- Sit in stillness and follow the breath
- Transcendental Meditation
- Guided meditations
- Walking meditation

Move:

- Stretch
- Do yoga
- Walk or run
- Work out
- Swim
- Ride a bike

- Do Chi Kung/Qi Gong or Tai Chi
- Dance
- Do some self-massage

Write:

- Journal, either in a notebook or on the computer
- Morning pages (from *The Artist's Way* by Julia Cameron)
- Creative writing

Quick/Easy:

- Stretch in bed before you get up, and take several deep breaths
- Pause as you get out of bed and feel your feet on the ground
- Drink your coffee or tea mindfully
- Shower mindfully
- Listen to music
- Read a poem
- Look at something that inspires you
- Go outside and pay attention
- Take three deep breaths
- Do a thirty-second or one-minute brain dump: write (or dictate into your phone) everything that is currently on your mind
- Look for things to appreciate
- Listen to an uplifting podcast while you drive to work or run errands
- Listen to a guided meditation on the way to work if you take public transportation
- Scan your body and breathe into any tense areas

Appendix 4
Questions for Reflection

During your morning ritual or at quiet moments in your day, contemplate these questions. It might be helpful to journal about them and write down anything that comes to mind, without thinking too much or editing yourself. Give yourself permission to speak freely.

What do I need?
What do I want?
What do I love?
What do I crave?
What do I yearn for?
What do I miss?
What am I most proud of?
What did I love to do when I was younger that I don't do anymore?
What am I tired of doing?
What do I want less of in my life?
What do I want more of in my life?
What are my favorite ways to treat myself?
How can I treat myself today?
How can I take better care of myself?
What makes me sad?
What makes me happy?
What would make me happy right now?

What would make me happy today?
What would make me happy this week?
What would make me happy this month?
What would make me happy this year?
What do I really want to say?
What do I know that I'm ignoring?
What am I afraid of?
What dreams have I put on hold?
What would my perfect day look like?
What does my dream life look like?

Appendix 5
Name What You What

Sometimes it can be difficult to figure out what you want, especially when your days are hectic. A morning ritual can provide the space to reflect on what you truly want your life to look like. The words below can help you pinpoint what's most important to you and how you want to feel in your ideal life.

Scan this list and see what words resonate with you. Write them down in your journal, then consider how you can incorporate these qualities into your life. Perhaps you can create affirmations that you read to yourself during your morning ritual. Maybe you can post the most important ones around your house.

Come back to this list from time to time and see if new words jump out at you. It can be very illuminating to do this exercise regularly.

Healthy
Energetic
Playful
Passionate
Giving
Calm
Peaceful
Happy
Conscious
Joyful
Exuberant
Mischievous
Centered
Grounded
Quiet
Content
Boisterous
Accomplished
Anticipatory
Cheerful
Dynamic
Attractive
Comfortable
Buoyant
Capable
Extraordinary
Compassionate
Committed
Available
Driven
Connected

Loving
Focused
Curious
Decisive
Dependable
Patient
Kind
Harmonious
Vital
Magical
Abundant
Creative
Brilliant
Contemplative
Enthusiastic
Accepted
Quiet
Consistent
Mindful
Graceful
Fun
Generous
Clean
Firm
Devoted
Aware
Frank
Close
Free
Lighthearted
Rich

Grateful
Playful
Efficient
Elated
Benevolent
Bold
Frugal
Appreciative
Assertive
Empathic
Diligent
Encouraging
Secure
Delighted
Thankful
Zesty
Soulful
Blissful
Fierce
Outlandish
Spunky
Poised
Easy
Relaxed
Spontaneous
Carefree
Open
Clear
Adventurous
Purposeful
Intuitive

Helpful	Exhilarated	Unique
Adaptable	Significant	Leading
Flexible	Family-oriented	Humorous
Agile	Satisfied	Imaginative
Clear-minded	Selfless	Logical
Dedicated	Popular	Impartial
Confident	Unflappable	Encouraged
Dignified	Trusting	Fascinated
Disciplined	Proactive	Precise
Dreaming	Self-reliant	Trustworthy
Effective	Mysterious	Industrious
Fearless	Sympathetic	Faithful
Friendly	Youthful	Eager
Attentive	Liberated	Dutiful
Awestruck	Understanding	Inquisitive
Balanced	Open	Optimistic
Brave	Motivated	Inspired
Careful	Loyal	Traditional
Integrity	Powerful	Exploring
Intimate	Sensitive	Fair
Inventive	Organized	Vital
Cooperative	Order	Tranquil
Determined	Lively	Neat
Independent	Sensual	Resourceful
Perceptive	Growing	Truthful
Persistent	Honest	Useful
Elegant	Prosperous	Just
Entertained	Reasonable	Warm
Guided	Hopeful	Learning
Excited	Sacred	Prudent
Insightful	Humble	Realistic

Loving	Polished	Stable
Mellow	Thoughtful	Simple
Serene	Prepared	Present
Wise	Spiritual	Witty
Sharing	Reliable	Privacy
Meticulous	Supportive	Strong
Open-minded	Resilient	Thrifty
Practical	Tough	Vivacious
Successful	Reverent	Wealthy
Variety	Silly	Tidy
Virtuous	Willing	Resolute
Supported	Solitary	Original
Thankful	Fit	Wonder-filled

Appendix 6
Affirmations

Below are some of the affirmations I created, which I read to myself each morning. I invite you to use any that resonate, or create your own.

I feel loved and am loving and kind and patient
with others, especially my husband and son.

I feel connected to others and foster a harmonious atmosphere.

I treasure my mental and physical
health and take care of myself.

I take delight in the world and feel
energetic, playful, and passionate.

I seek joy and pleasure each day.

I am open to a variety of experiences that fill
me with wonder, exuberance, and vitality.

I welcome outrageousness, magic, unexpected
surprises, and chances for fun adventure!

I'm guided by my intuition toward a healthy, happy
life with beloved family and dear friends, filled
with abundance, creative endeavors, and fun!

I go with the flow.

I have all the time I need to do what I want.

Resources

If you would like to join the *Beautiful Morning* Community (a closed Facebook group) to share your experiences, encourage others, and enjoy support as you implement your morning ritual, email me at Ashley@abeautifulmorningbook.com. You can also sign up for my mailing list at www.abeautifulmorningbook.com.

Recommended reading

*Books that are particularly suited for reading during your morning ritual

Personal Development/Happiness

Gift from the Sea, Anne Morrow Lindbergh*
The Joy Diet, Martha Beck*
The Miracle of Mindfulness, Thich Nhat Hanh*
Peace Is Every Step, Thich Nhat Hanh*
Being Perfect, Anna Quindlen*
A Short Guide to a Happy Life, Anna Quindlen*
How to Live a Good Life, Jonathan Fields*
*Wake Up to the Joy of You: 52 Meditations and Practices for a
      Calmer, Happier Life*, Agapi Stassinopoulos*
Luzy Lessons, Wendy Battino*
May Cause Miracles, Gabrielle Bernstein*
Finding Your Way in a Wild New World, Martha Beck
Diana, Herself, Martha Beck
Expecting Adam, Martha Beck
The Gifts of Imperfection, Brené Brown

Daring Greatly, Brené Brown
Rising Strong, Brené Brown
Braving the Wilderness, Brené Brown
The Happiness Project, Gretchen Rubin
Happier at Home, Gretchen Rubin
Better than Before, Gretchen Rubin
The Four Tendencies, Gretchen Rubin
Eat, Pray, Love, Elizabeth Gilbert
How We Choose to Be Happy, Rick Foster and Greg Hicks
Live What You Love, Bob and Melinda Blanchard
Life Reimagined, Barbara Bradley Hagerty
The 52 Weeks, Karen Amster-Young and Pam Godwin
The Book of Joy, His Holiness the Dalai Lama, Archbishop
　　　Desmond Tutu, and Douglas Abrams
Loving What Is, Byron Katie
A Return to Love, Marianne Williamson
Dying to Be Me, Anita Moorjani
The Power of Now, Eckhart Tolle
The Desire Map, Danielle LaPorte
Outrageous Openness, Tosha Silver
There's Not Enough Time … and Other Lies We Tell Ourselves,
　　　Jill Farmer
The Miracle Morning, Hal Elrod
The Lotus and the Lily, Janet Conner
When Your Superpower Becomes Your Kryptonite, Tracey Hewitt

Personal Development/Creativity/Art

The Artist's Way, Julia Cameron
Vein of Gold, Julia Cameron

Big Magic, Elizabeth Gilbert
Drawing on the Right Side of the Brain, Betty Edwards
Paint Mojo: Creative Layering Techniques for Personal Expression,
     Tracy Verdugo
The Zen of Seeing, Frederick Franck
Zen Seeing, Zen Drawing: Meditation in Action,
     Frederick Franck

Poetry

New and Selected Poems, Volume One, Mary Oliver*
A Thousand Mornings: Poems, Mary Oliver*
Why I Wake Early: New Poems, Mary Oliver*
Felicity: Poems, Mary Oliver*
The Essential Rumi, translation by Coleman Barks*

Mindfulness/Meditation

Tao Te Ching, Lao Tzu, translated by Stephen Mitchell*
*Wherever You Go, There You Are: Mindfulness Meditation in
     Everyday Life*, Jon Kabat-Zinn*
*Wake Up to the Joy of You: 52 Meditations and Practices for a
     Calmer, Happier Life*, Agapi Stassinopoulos*
Bunny Buddhism: Hopping Along the Path to Enlightenment,
     Krista Lester*
May Cause Miracles, Gabrielle Bernstein*
Easy Now, Jocelyn Cates

You can find live links to much of the information below at
www.abeautifulmorningbook.com/resources.

More information on the women featured in this book

Wendy Battino: www.wendybattino.com
Martha Beck: www.marthabeck.com
Patricia Charpentier: www.writingyourlife.org
Christie Federico: www.christiefederico.com
Karen "KJ Sassypants" Hawkwood:
        www.deepclaritycoaching.com
Anna Kunnecke: www.declaredominion.com
Lezlie Laws: www.lezlielaws.com
Tonya Lewis Lee: www.healthyyounow.com /
        www.movitaorganics.com
Cynthia Morris: www.originalimpulse.com
Carla Robertson: www.livingwildandprecious.com
Holly Shoebridge: www.hollytreephoto.com
Koelle Simpson: www.koelleinstitute.com
Sonia Sommer: www.soniasommer.com
Tracy Verdugo: www.tracyverdugo.com
Keri Wilt: www.fhbandme.com
Stacy Wooster: www.stacywooster.com

Websites and apps

Websites:

Creativebug (over 1,000 video classes on a vast array of creative
        arts): www.creativebug.com
The Good Life Project (focused on helping people live more
        meaningful lives; also host Camp GLP, a grown-up

summer camp each August in New York):
www.goodlifeproject.com

Lucky Star Art Camp (annual retreat for women, held each
November in the Texas Hill Country):
www.luckystarartcamp.com

750words (private writing website; helps you track your writing and also provides analysis): www.750words.com

Devotional apps:

Daily Hope
D365
Holy Bible
Jesus Calling
3 Minute Retreat
P31: First 5

Meditation apps:

Abraham-Hicks Getting into the Vortex
Calm
Headspace
Insight Timer
The Mindfulness App
Sattva
Smiling Mind

Materials and practices mentioned in this book

[The links below are provided for informative purposes only and are not meant to promote any particular website or group.—Author]

Bulletproof coffee: https://blog.bulletproof.com/
Chi Kung/Qi Gong: https://en.wikipedia.org/wiki/Qigong
Daily Compass, Queen Sweep: www.declaredominion.com
Five-Year Journal: www.writingyourlife.org/shop/
        five-year-journal/
Kolbe Index: www.kolbe.com/assessments/
Liquid Mind music: www.liquidmindmusic.com
Meditation: https://zenhabits.net/meditation-guide/
        https://www.gaiam.com/blogs/discover/meditation
           -101-techniques-benefits-and-a-beginner
           -s-how-to
Modeh Ani prayer:http://www.chabad.org/library/article_cdo/
        aid/623937/jewish/Modeh-Ani.htm
Money Love Program by Kate Northrup:
        http://katenorthrup.com/money-love-resources/
TIA Method journal: not available at press time; please check
        www.abeautifulmorningbook.com/resources
Transcendental Meditation: www.tm.org
Vipassana Meditation: https://www.lionsroar.com/
        how-to-practice-vipassana-insight-meditation/
The Work of Byron Katie: www.thework.com
Write into Light: http://marthabeck.com/
        wil-first-to-know-2018

Acknowledgments

I am immensely grateful to all of the amazing women who participated in this project; thank you for helping me bring it to life so vividly. I'm especially thankful to Martha Beck for providing years of transformative revelations through her words, thus helping me get to this point, and for creating the Write into Light course, which opened the portal for this idea and strengthened my ability to see it through.

Thank you, thank you to Carla Robertson for encouraging me along the way and being my first interview, and to Cynthia Morris for being both an interviewee and my book coach; your enthusiasm and creative thinking were invaluable! Thank you also to Tanja Richter for cheering me on and helping keep me sane.

Enormous gratitude to all my early readers for your extremely helpful comments: Tracey Hewitt, Annie Ferguson Moscato, Lauren Oujiri, Michelle Pattridge, Carla Robertson, Susan Telford, Jessica Dunne Waite, and Mary Walker. Thank you, Mary, for your brilliant suggestions of the breaks between chapters and the permission slip! Jody Berman, I deeply appreciate your careful and insightful editing.

Thank you to the incredible women in Kate Northrup's Origin group who gave me valuable cover feedback and shared their morning rituals, and to fellow writers in the ALLi (Alliance of Independent Authors) online forum who also provided excellent feedback on the cover. Holly Shoebridge, thank you for your bright spirit and gorgeous photography! Damon, Alisha, Chrissy, and Benjamin of Damonza, your design work exceeded my expectations; you made my book look so lovely. Evelyn Laws Savage, thank you for working your photographic magic on me.

I couldn't have done this without my glorious tribe of Lightwriting sisters, who lifted me up at every turn with encouragement and inspiration.

Finally, the biggest thank-you of all to my family; your unwavering love, patience, and support made this possible, and I'm beyond lucky to have you.

About the Author

Ashley Ellington Brown grew up in New Orleans and graduated from the University of Virginia with a degree in foreign affairs (which she did not use, although she had a lot of fun getting it). She worked as a waitress, receptionist, advertising copywriter and account executive, book editor, and employee communications manager for the world's third-largest death-care firm before becoming a freelance writer in 2000. This is her first book. Ashley lives in Florida with her husband and son and their rescued beagle, Snoopy.

Made in the USA
Middletown, DE
08 April 2020

87981462R00125